"I am very excited about how God is going to use this book for his glory! Daniel began an orphan care ministry in our church by inviting interested families to join him for Bible studies on the topic of God's heart for orphans. God worked through those studies to produce a passion for the fatherless in the hearts of many of our families. Each Sunday I look upon smiling faces of little children who now have homes where they are loved and are being taught the gospel of Jesus."

Ritch Boerckel
Senior Pastor, Bethany Baptist Church

"*A Passion for the Fatherless* puts the gospel right where it should be, namely, at the very center of the global orphan crisis. If the church is to faithfully fulfill the orphan mandate, the gospel must be at the center of both the church's motivation for and its practice of orphan care. This book is a must read for everyone who wants the church of Jesus Christ to lead the way in caring for our world's orphans."

Dan Cruver,
Director of Together for Adoption

"I am delighted to see such a strong emphasis on a theology of the fatherless in Dan's book. It is truly the heart beat of our heavenly Father and such a great need in our world today. This book will help inspire and equip God's people to be more fully engaged in loving the orphan."

John Fuder
Professor of Urban Studies, Moody Theological Seminary

"Daniel Bennett addresses an evangelical church that is reawakening to its social responsibilities. A particular strength of his work is that it does not make the usual emotional appeals. Instead, it is grounded in Scripture and sound theology which bring about lasting commitment to the task."

Dan Green
Professor, Moody Theological Seminary

"This work does the adoption and orphan ministry community a significant service by filling the theological gap between God-given compassion and practical application. It helps guide those important decisions about starting, structuring, and keeping momentum going in compassion ministries. *A Passion for the Fatherless* is an enjoyable read that's marked with Bennett's subtle humor as he lays a firm foundation for a new generation of adoptive parents and leaders in orphan ministries and provides an insightful refresher for those of us who are already serving in the trenches. I highly recommend it!"

Jodi Lewis,
Lay Leader, Orphan and Adoption Ministry

"This book is based on a careful study of what the Bible has to say about orphan care (and the answer, is plenty!), and why we cannot ignore the most helpless and abandoned of God's creation without grieving the heart of God. All who are in Christian ministry should read it and ask: How should we get involved?"

—Dr. Erwin Lutzer,
Senior Pastor, Moody Church

"In my position I read heart-wrenching stories about the plight of orphans on a regular basis. You know what I like about this book? Daniel Bennett takes the emotional concern that we should have for the orphan and puts it in clear biblical perspective. The glory of God as relates to the value of children—especially fatherless and motherless children—are at the heart of this book. That in and of itself should take the matter beyond a superficial emotion response to deliberate compassionate action on the part of believers. You cannot read this book and feel otherwise."

—Marvin Newell,
Executive Director, CrossGlobal Link

"The number of orphans in the world staggers the imagination. In light of these overwhelming physical and spiritual needs, what would God have his church to do, and how are we to do it? In *A Passion for the Fatherless*, Daniel Bennett takes readers on an engaging theological journey, instructing them how to answer these questions with biblical faithfulness and practical wisdom."

—Robert L. Plummer,
Associate Professor of New Testament Interpretation
The Southern Baptist Theological Seminary

"*A Passion for the Fatherless* boldly sums up the great doctrines of the gospel and adoption. Daniel Bennett has rightly captured the call for God's children to illustrate our Father's longing to welcome, embrace, and place into his family we who were spiritually alone and fatherless."

—Mark A. Tatlock
Senior Vice President and Provost, The Master's College

"Daniel Bennett is a man who loves Christ, his word, his people, and his concerns. This book springs from those loves and is a worthy read by all believers."

William Thrasher
Professor, Moody Theological Seminary

A Passion *for the* Fatherless

Developing a God-Centered Ministry to Orphans

DANIEL J. BENNETT

Kregel
Academic & Professional

Library of Congress Cataloging-in-Publication Data
Bennett, Daniel J., 1977-
    A passion for the fatherless : developing a God-centered ministry to orphans / Daniel J. Bennett.
        p. cm.
    Includes bibliographical references (p. 219) and indexes.
    1. Church work with orphans. I. Title.
    BV4464.4.B46 2011
    261.8'3273—dc22

                                                                    2011002363

978-0-8254-2660-5

Printed in the United States of America
11 12 13 14 15 / 5 4 3 2 1

To Whitney,
my friend and partner in life and ministry

CONTENTS

FOREWORD

In a space not much larger than my daughters' bedroom, some twenty babies lay in cribs, tended by two caring but overwhelmed orphanage workers. One particular child I'll never forget. Her face appeared to be about two years old, but her arms and legs resembled twigs, apparently the result of spending virtually every hour of every day on her back. Picking her up, I found her diaper and ragged clothing were saturated—several times over, it seemed. The stench and moisture soaking into my shirt stung my senses, making me want to lay her down immediately. But I couldn't, and tried to hold her close like I did my own two-year-old. When I finally set her down, we both cried. I'd come to the country to bring home a different orphan, my adopted daughter. But I was overcome in that moment by how many would remain behind.

That same month, a girl who'd grown up in the U.S. foster system was nearing the end of high school. Less than half of foster youth graduate, but she'd overcome the odds and earned her diploma. As graduation approached, however, she expressed no desire to walk the stage. Encouraged, cajoled, and finally begged by her social worker, she refused again and again. Finally, she confessed, "I don't want to go because I'll be the only one up there with no one in the audience to clap for me."

From the other side of the world to the other side of the tracks, the needs of the fatherless are vast. Latest estimates put the number of orphans globally at 163 million. All of these children have lost a mother or father; about 10 percent have lost both. In the United States, roughly 425,000 children live in the foster system at any given time, with about 115,000 currently waiting to be adopted.

The details of these children's lives vary greatly, but most all represent the "fatherless" that God repeatedly calls his people to defend. They are the orphans in distress, whose care James describes as the heart of pure religion. The majority face the world without provider or protector, encountering apathy on one side and predators on the other.

Yet what is one person to do? To survey the entirety of the need is crushing. To see it in the bloodshot eyes of the single little boy who again cried himself to sleep upon the grave of his mother is sorrowful beyond

9

measure. And although duty or guilt or idealism can spur us to mount a fevered response, these motivations alone will ultimately prove unequal to the task. The vast need will almost certainly outstrip our enthusiasm to address it.

In the face of this reality, what hope remains? Is there any motivation sufficient for the scope of the problem? Is there community that, joined together, can foster and support the perseverance required? Is there any reason to think that what little we have to offer could really make a lasting difference?

Daniel Bennett helps us see the answer to these questions. It is not merely a mumbled affirmation, but a booming *yes!*

There *is* sufficient motivation, so deep it will never run dry; for we worship a God who pursued us when we were destitute and alone. He adopted us as his children and invites us to call him *Abba*. We merely mirror his heart when we seek out and serve the fatherless. It is not guilt or duty or idealism alone, but the love of Christ that compels us. Truly, we love because he first loved us.

There *is* also community sufficient to help us persevere: the local church. Foster care, adoption, and global orphan ministry will always be best when we engage not as lone crusaders but as part of a band of believers. We need encouragers, supporters, and practical aid amidst the beauty and pain we are certain to encounter along this path. From conversations and encounters I have almost daily, I can attest that churches are indeed rising to this role; Daniel Bennett's church has, and countless others have as well. To a watching world, there may be no more powerful apologetic than to see communities of believers standing together for the fatherless.

With a view of the whole, we begin to realize what a profound difference each of us can make. Some foster. Some adopt. Some mentor. Some give foster families respite. Some support adoptions financially. Some aid churches overseas in caring for orphans in their own communities. As we each exercise our unique gifts in unison, the paralyzing statics of overwhelming need fade to the background. We see the single statistic that matters more than any other: it takes only *one* caring individual to make a lifelong difference for an orphan.

Every week, I encounter more churches that have caught this vision. Often, it is initiated by one couple or a few friends who've been awoken to God's heart for the fatherless. And bit by bit, in fits and starts, they grow a community committed to making the gospel visible in loving care for the orphan.

The deeper we look, the more we realize that this vision is not only about transforming the lives of orphans. As one woman who helps

Christians engage the foster system in Arkansas expressed, "I see these kids changed—but I think the parents are changed even more." God is using the great need of orphans to address the greatest need of the church also. In loving orphans, we are pulled beyond flaccid and uninspiring religion to a muscular faith of gospel-motivated sacrifice and gospel-rooted joy.

This is the road Daniel Bennett invites us on together. It may well cost you more than the price of this book, but I daresay it will be worth every penny. For loving the orphan in distress is ultimately a discipleship journey. As with all of God's summons, it demands of us things we'd rather not lose; yet it also carries more purpose and deeper joy than we could find at the best golf course or finest day spa. If that's what you desire, venture on!

JEDD MEDEFIND
President, Christian Alliance for Orphans

PREFACE

The purpose of this book is to expose believers to the scriptural mandate to care for orphans, to help them understand why God has issued that call, and to equip them to joyfully respond. It strives to achieve this purpose by developing a vibrant theology of orphan ministry for the church.

The idea for this book began as our church's orphan ministry looked for a Bible study. We found that there was a lack of material that took solid, God-centered teaching and applied it to the ministry of caring for the fatherless. While much had been written concerning adoption, we saw a need for a work that was more comprehensive.

In 2007 we began a small group Bible study that sought to meet this need, and God used his Word powerfully in the hearts of the people in our church, calling them to a variety of orphan care ministries. Some have worked at orphanages, some have adopted, some have been called to be foster parents, many to pray, and some to financially support those who adopt. We are grateful that we have had the opportunity to apply God's truth and for what he has done in the life of our church as a result.

How to Use This Book

A Passion for the Fatherless consists of three parts. Part 1, God and the Orphan, focuses on understanding the character of God and his ministry to the orphan. Part 2, God's People and the Orphan, explores how those who have been transformed by the miracle of spiritual adoption are called by God to care for the orphan. Part 3, Beginning an Orphan Ministry in Your Church, focuses more on the nuts and bolts issues of orphan care ministry.

Throughout the book, I have included stories to illustrate biblical principles. The stories are real-life examples of how God has worked in the lives of his saints.

Study Groups

The book is written with both individuals and small groups in mind. If you decide to go through the book with a group, the chapters in parts 1 and

2 contain study questions that are designed to help stimulate discussion on the subjects presented in the chapter. When you meet as a group, you can discuss the questions and any additional insights on the themes presented.

If possible, make sure that there is a strong teacher as the group facilitator. The facilitator should get a firm grasp on the concepts in the chapter and come to the study group with an outline for the session. The facilitator may want to prepare a devotional based upon one of the passages in the chapter and determine the best pace to go through the book.

As important as I believe communicating biblical principles are, I am also convinced that you must make sure that there is time to build relationships within the group. Perhaps you can bring some snacks to allow a time for people to fellowship beforehand. Each session should begin with a time of prayer for one another. The couples and individuals in your church may be embarking on one of the most challenging times of their lives. They need to have a network of saints to whom they can turn when they encounter various hardships. The people from the orphan care study can be a great source of spiritual and emotional support.

Contrary to what your mother taught you, be sure to "scratch what itches." I provide a suggested overview for small group discussion at the end of each chapter, but you may find that the concerns of the group go beyond the topics raised there. It can be helpful to allow some moderated "rabbit trails," especially toward the end of the time together.

Beginning an Orphan Care Ministry

The third part of the book is for people who are trying to begin an orphan ministry in their churches or improve an existing one. An orphan care ministry can be defined as *the spirit-empowered efforts of God's family to meet the physical and spiritual needs of the orphan.* This definition is intentionally broad and encompasses a range of ministries such as the following:

- Adoption (domestic and foreign)
- Adoption funding
- Foster parenting
- Prayer ministry
- Childcare
- Working at an orphanage
- Short-term mission trips

The goal is that through the study of the first two parts, you will have a greater sense of how God may be calling you and your church to use your unique gifts to meet these needs. The third part of the book deals with issues such as how to how to approach church leaders to begin an orphan ministry, small steps to beginning the ministry, and determining the components of your church's orphan ministry.

Encouraging Pastors

When talking with individuals about orphan care ministry, perhaps the most frequent question I get is related to how to help church leaders capture the vision of caring for orphans. This book has also been designed for individuals to give to their pastors or other church leaders. Be careful regarding your expectations, however. As a senior pastor, every few weeks someone gives me a book to read. I enjoy reading those books, but I also appreciate the freedom to read through them at my own pace!

ACKNOWLEDGMENTS

There are numerous people who deserve recognition for their contributions to the writing of this book. Let me name just a few of them. First and foremost is my wife, Whitney, who shouldered the responsibilities of being not just a pastor's wife but an author's wife as well for several months. The kids—Hannah, Austin, Noah, and Ellie—were also gracious with their dad's time. I love you, and it is a privilege to be a part of your family.

Dad, Mom, Andrew, Matthew, and Emily gave me an early understanding of what a beautiful thing a family can be and, more importantly, how precious the family of God is.

Ritch Boerckel, Lyall Sutton, and Fred Laugherty mentored me when I arrived at Bethany Baptist in August 2000, and they continue to be faithful in ministry there. I am especially grateful to Ritch, who has influenced me as my youth pastor, my senior pastor, and my friend.

The people in the congregations that make up the Bethany Fellowship of Churches have been a great joy to me and my family. I am thankful for the opportunity to work with Ritch and my friend Art Georges at Living Hope Community Church.

It is difficult to express how blessed my family is to serve at Bethany Community Church. The congregation loves the Lord and his Word and is passionate for his glory—and we love them deeply! The lay elders—Tony Carbaugh, Mark DeJarnatt, Craig Hodges, Kent Kloter, Kevin Martin, and Dave Robinson—are committed to the task of shepherding. The staff—Pastor Ben Davidson, Worship Minister Mike Chambers, and our office manager Diane Geurin—are faithful colaborers for the gospel.

Jack Kragt's passion for orphans is contagious, and without his encouragement this book would never have come into existence. Jim Weaver and Kregel Publications have been very gracious for allowing me this opportunity. Dawn Anderson, my editor at Kregel, made my words clearer, and Paul Hillman guided me through the publishing process. I hope that God is glorified through Kregel's ministry to the evangelical community.

There are numerous others who deserve recognition, such as Andy Lehman at Lifesong for Orphans and Jedd Medefind at Christian Alliance for Orphans, for the work they have done for our orphan care ministry. I am also thankful to the many of you who shared your stories with me and gave me feedback at various stages of the project.

Finally, a special thanks to Chuck Boysen, Michelle Hahn, Monica Lonergan, Amy Park, Jerry Sanderson, and Lisa Schwarz, who serve on the Open Hearts, Open Homes committee. Their compassion for the fatherless has blessed our church in ways that I am sure will not be fully comprehended until eternity.

INTRODUCTION

What is the relationship between theology and having compassion for the fatherless? At first glance, they may appear to be unrelated. Theologians dwell in the land of academia, and their hands are smooth. Those who engage in caring for the fatherless have callused hands; they strive to accomplish something useful.

Let me suggest to you, however, that theology and orphan care ministry in the church are inextricably linked. Without a knowledge of who God is—theology—it is impossible to know what he desires us to do. As people know God more fully, their ability to understand his will increases. As they understand him and his will more fully, they experience greater joy in their ministry. As their joy in ministry increases, God receives more glory. Therefore, unless believers understand the heart of God again—theology for the fatherless—their efforts at ministry will be severely hampered.

I have not been lost in a car since November of 2008. That was the month in which our family was given a GPS navigation device. With this little miracle machine we always know where we are going and how to get there. If I begin to go the wrong way, a very friendly and slightly annoying voice begins to suggest that I make a U-turn as soon as possible. In a similar way, instead of being completely distinct from and irrelevant for our daily lives, theology is like a navigation device. It helps us understand where we are, where we need to go, and the pathway we take to get there. When we are out of line, it prods us to get back on the right path.

My compassion for orphans flows from the fact that I know God and know that he passionately cares for the fatherless. I love orphans because I love God. If I did not have this theological understanding, my passion for orphans would be commendable but ultimately worthless.

How Our Church Became
Passionate About Orphans

The story of how our church's orphan ministry began illustrates the crucial link between theology and ministry. In the summer of 2005, while serving as a family pastor, I began to notice the effective ministry foster parents were having. They were opening up their homes to children, bringing them to church, and having great conversations with them about their relationship with Jesus Christ. I was stunned to find out that parents were even paid to minister to these children. Believers were being assisted by the state to do something God had commanded them to do! I began to pray that God would give our church a vision for caring for foster children.

As I was thinking through what this ministry might look like, I received a providential call from Andy Lehman, the vice-president of Lifesong for Orphans. He was trying to connect with local churches to discuss his organization's ministry. We met at a Chinese buffet and talked for several hours. Andy expanded my vision for the ministry from simply caring for foster children to ministering to orphans worldwide. I left our lunch quite full of both Chinese food and excitement for our future ministry.

For several months, I studied what the Bible said about the fatherless and considered a variety of ways our church could be obedient to God's Word. This study took me from believing that orphan care would be a good ministry to do to believing that it was a ministry our church must do.

As I talked with a few people at our church about the possible ministry, I found that God had already been working within the hearts of his saints. Many had been thinking about what an orphan ministry could look like before I talked with them. An adoption committee was formed to help us take the first few baby steps. They began to work on establishing the ministry and soon outpaced my initial efforts. We advertised a few meetings to gauge interest and developed a mission statement and a general understanding of what we would try to do with the ministry. We finally came to the point where I felt like we were ready to approach the leaders with a plan and officially launch an orphan ministry.

Remember, I had been spending *months* thinking through the ministry and studying biblical texts that dealt with how to care for the fatherless. The plan I compiled, however, focused more on the practical aspects of how to implement those biblical principles at our church than the principles themselves. It was light on theology and heavy on pragmatics. Oh, I threw in a verse here and there at the beginning (James 1:27, of course), but there was no sustained biblical explanation of God's passion for the fatherless.

I went into that first meeting with the elders with high (unrealistic) expectations. I believed that the elders would simply declare my proposal the most brilliant document they had ever seen and we'd begin immediately. Perhaps there would even be talk about declaring me associate pastor of the year. Certainly there would be no dissent. All the bases were covered. The proposal could not be improved upon.

At the meeting, I quickly quoted a few Bible verses then launched into the presentation. I talked about areas of need, how our church could meet them, how financial contributions could be made, the mission trips we would take, etc., etc. Then I sat back and waited for the applause. In my imagination, one of the elders leapt to his feet, jumped on the table, and declared, "This must be done post-haste!"

The real response was more lackluster; no one disagreed with the notion of caring for orphans. In fact, everyone was pretty much in agreement that children should be cared for—especially the fatherless. The questions the elders asked indicated a concern for orphans but confusion as to the responsibility of the church corporately. What level and type of involvement should the local church have? Had not other families pursued this ministry without the backing of the church? What were the disadvantages of the church getting involved? Why focus on all the areas I had proposed, such as international adoption? Why not simply focus our efforts on the fatherless in our own community? Why should we as a church support this ministry financially instead of letting individual couples do this? Did we have enough resources to accomplish this ministry? The elders asked me to consider these questions and come back again with a revised proposal.

When I left the meeting, I wondered why the group as a whole had not had the same excitement for my proposal that I had. Three thoughts came to mind. First, it was their job to think through details, and their questions did not necessarily mean a lack of desire to do the ministry. Second, my excitement for orphan ministry had evolved over time; I could not expect our elders to become excited about a ministry after thinking about it for just a few minutes. Third, and related to the second thought, I realized I had become so wrapped up in how to do the ministry, I had forgotten why I had become so passionate about orphan care in the first place. My focus on the practical parts of the ministry had led me to neglect the theological elements. Their questions had been responses to what I had presented. There had been what I perceived as a lack of passion because I had failed to give them the biblical principles to rally behind and become enthusiastic about helping our church apply.

I came back to the next meeting with the answers to the questions that had been raised, but before addressing these, I spent a good deal of time talking about the biblical principles regarding orphan care. Being spiritually mature men, they had a good grasp of the concepts this study addressed. I tried to take what they already knew and show the biblical applications to orphan ministry.

The elders were unanimously excited about being obedient to God in this area as they saw how his Word was passionate about this ministry. The proposal was approved—although I still never heard the word "brilliant" used in reference to it—and our church began a new phase in its ministry to the fatherless.

Perhaps your church or individuals within your church need to develop that passion as well. My hope is that this book helps believers develop a passion for the fatherless that is rooted in God's Word and allows them to pursue the care of children with joy.

The Necessity of This Study

With the story of our church in mind, let me suggest four reasons why I believe this book is so necessary.

We Must Do the Right Things for the Right Reasons

First, this book is necessary because believers must do the right things for the right reasons. As a pastor, my job is not simply to motivate people to do ministry. It is to motivate people to do ministry for God-glorifying reasons. If I desire to motivate people to work in the nursery, I could stand up in the pulpit and plead with them. I could remind them how much they owe God. I could tell them, with tears streaming down my face, that surely they can pay God back by serving just a few hours a week helping the precious little children. Using shame and coercion, I could get people to do what I believe is the right thing for them to do.

Such an effort, I believe, would not be God-honoring. I desire people to serve God, not because they are shamed into ministry but because they have a God-given delight in it. Paul labored hard in ministry, but it was not ultimately him who labored but the "grace of God" working within him (1 Cor. 15:10). As God equips and enables, he rightly receives credit for the work that is done. I stand culpable before God not only for the type of ministry the people in the church are involved in but also why they are engaged in it. Therefore, this book is concerned that people develop a passion not for the fatherless, first and foremost, but for God.

Children Are in Need

Second, this book is necessary because children are in need. There are several seemingly contradictory estimates regarding the number of orphans worldwide. The United Nations Children's Fund (UNICEF) estimates that there are currently more than 132 million orphaned children.[1] A few words, however, should be said about UNICEF's orphan estimates.

---

1. UNICEF, "Orphans."

UNICEF defines an orphan as "a child who has lost one or both parents." This would mean that a child who still has a surviving parent, or is living with his or her grandparents or other extended relatives, is considered an orphan.

If one were to define an orphan as a child who has lost both of his or her parents—a "double orphan"—UNICEF estimates that 13 million of the 132 million orphaned children fit that definition. Of these 13 million double orphans, a still smaller percentage are available for adoption.

The church must help their people gain an understanding of how they can be involved in meeting the needs of all orphans, not just those who are "adoptable." Most of the current resources being produced by the church are focused on adoption and not orphan care. Adoption is easier to understand than other forms of orphan care ministry, is sometimes less messy, and the stories are often more heartwarming.

We certainly need resources to equip the church to engage in the ministry of adoption, but we must simultaneously realize that orphan care ministry is far bigger than we can imagine. UNICEF is right when it expresses concern that too narrowly defining who is an orphan may "lead to responses that focus on providing care for individual children rather than supporting the families and communities that care for orphans and are in need of support."[2] In other words, the church needs to understand that the needs of orphans in the world cannot be met only by adopting children—though that is an important component. The church must understand that there is an overwhelming need to which Christ's church has an opportunity to respond.

Christians Are Not Thinking Biblically About Caring for Orphans

Third, this book is necessary because Christians are not thinking biblically about caring for orphans. Sometimes, our "biblical" defense for orphan care goes no further than quoting James 1:27: "Religion that is pure and undefiled before God, the Father, is this: to visit orphans and widows in their affliction, and to keep oneself unstained from the world."

But what is James saying? What does he mean by "pure religion"? What is the relationship between pure religion and caring for the disenfranchised? Does Scripture have more to teach us regarding how and why to care for the fatherless?

I would contend that our lack of consideration of Scripture's teaching regarding orphans is symptomatic of the overall malaise within the church

---

2. Ibid.

toward theology. Theology has all but disappeared in many Christian circles. This is not to say that Christians are vigorously campaigning against theology. The attack has been far more subtle. Theology's disappearance, as David Wells puts it,

> is not the same as the abduction of a child who is happily playing at home one minute and then is no longer to be found the next. No one has abducted theology in this sense. The disappearance is closer to what happens in homes where the children are ignored and, to all intents and purposes, abandoned. They remain in the home, but they have no place in the family. So it is with theology in the Church. It remains on the edges of evangelical life, but it has been dislodged from its center.[3]

Theology's removal was not malicious, but its effects have been disastrous. Many believers live and minister without being quite sure why. They are like a child laughing at a joke and pretending to share in the amusement even though he does not quite understand the cause of the merriment. Christians give a good show at doing the right things even if they are not quite sure why they are so important.

Theology, our navigation device, is indispensable for staying on the right path. Unfortunately, a wedge is being driven between theology and living. Theology is viewed suspiciously. It is seen as the domain of deceased scholars who hypocritically pontificate from their coffins. Living, by contrast, is what those who are really connected with God do. Those who are focused on God are not as concerned with being right or with obscure theological debates, it is contended. They are instead consumed with experiencing God and being his ambassadors here as they participate in his kingdom. Which would you rather have, the argument goes, merely knowledge about God or a relationship with God? Would you rather do theology or ministry?

This is a false dichotomy and certainly not one God forces us into. Christians, unfortunately, are under the impression they cannot be both theological and practical. This sentiment is expressed in many different ways in contemporary evangelicalism. In seminary, I was walking across campus with a good friend, and we began talking about a paper we had been assigned. He told me, "Look, I'm not here to study and make good grades. I'm just here to love Jesus." I thought that was an astounding statement. Can

---

3. Wells, *No Place for Truth*, 106. For an updated look at the evangelical theological landscape, see Wells's *The Courage to Be Protestant*.

you imagine a student at med school saying, "Look, I'm not here to learn about medicine. I'm just here to help people get well"?

Forcing one to choose between living in relationship with God and knowing about God is unbiblical because the two are intricately connected in Scripture. Notice how Moses, as he speaks to the children of Israel, connects knowledge with how to live properly: "And now, O Israel, listen to the statutes and the rules that I am teaching you, and do them, that you may live" (Deut. 4:1).

Poor theology results in idolatry. The one who does not know the God of Scripture must fashion a god for himself. Moses therefore exhorts the Israelites to "take care, and keep your soul diligently, lest you forget the things that your eyes have seen, and lest they depart from your heart all the days of your life. Make them known to your children and your children's children" (Deut. 4:9). His fear is that the Israelites might be tempted to worship a false god if they forget the true God. He makes an impassioned plea for sound theology: "Since you saw no form on the day that the LORD spoke to you at Horeb out of the midst of the fire, beware lest you act corruptly by making a carved image for yourselves, in the form of any figure" (Deut. 4:15–16).

In contrast to the idolater, those with a right understanding of the one true God have the ability to worship him. As they do so, they demonstrate to those around them that they have a personal relationship with God. Reflecting his character as we practice his Word is a sign that our God is near.

Theology is not destructive to the Christian life, nor is it incidental. It is a navigational system that guides us as we strive to live as God has called us to live. If we fail to know God, we run the danger of practicing idolatry as we fashion gods in our own image. The choice we must make is not between knowing God or having a relationship with him. The real choice is between knowing God or practicing idolatry.

The Church Lacks Teaching Resources

Fourth, this book is necessary because the church needs tools to help train its people to care for orphans. There are not an abundance of materials that apply a theological understanding of the purpose of life and the nature of the church to the ministry of orphan care. There are some excellent resources that address the importance of adoption and some that even deal with the more pragmatic aspects of pursuing adoption. But the focus of this book is unique in that it gives a biblical understanding of several issues surrounding the church's care for the fatherless.

I mentioned earlier that according to some estimates there are well over 100 million orphans in the world. That is a staggering number. It is also an overwhelming opportunity. Christ's church can experience joy as she engages in ministry to the fatherless. This study combines a theological understanding of the church with a practical understanding of orphan ministry. It is designed to lay out a biblical and theological understanding of the nature of orphan ministry in the church so that it can do the right things for the right reasons.

One final thought. Tragedy is a theme in every orphan's story. It is a terrible thing that causes a child to be separated from her parents. Though I love all of my children, our child who was adopted, Ellie, touches my heart in a unique way. There are emotions that are stirred up as I look into her deep, brown eyes that I would never have felt if we had not had the blessing of her in our lives. There is a sorrow in my heart as I mourn the fact that she will probably never know her biological parents. I am writing these words on her third birthday, and my wife and I have mourned as we have thought about the pain her birth mother may be feeling today.

In the midst of tragedy, there is a far greater joy. Every time I tuck Ellie in at night, I am overwhelmed with thankfulness to the Lord. If it was his plan to not allow her to know her biological mother, I am grateful beyond words that he allowed Whitney and me to be the ones to bring her into our home to raise her. As I write this book, my desire is that others experience the joy of the Lord as we have. That does not mean that every person reading this should adopt or work at an orphanage. It means that I hope every person will become a passionate advocate for the fatherless in whatever way God calls them.

This study is ultimately for God, so that he will receive glory from the faithful ministry of his saints. It is secondarily a labor of love in my daughter Ellie's honor. It is my prayer that other little Ellies in the world will be taken care of as God works in the hearts of his adopted children.

PART ONE

God
and the
Orphan

For the Christian, understanding orphan care ministry begins by understanding the character of God. God passionately cares for the fatherless and has a unique purpose for our lives that should influence why we are motivated to care for orphans. That purpose is his glory. In fact, his compassion for the orphan flows from his passion for his glory. In part 1, we will see that the grace of God is proclaimed in a unique way as we provide for the fatherless.

1 The Uniqueness *of* Christian Orphan Care

Whitney and I made our way down the stony steps from our hotel room toward the lobby. It had not seemed so far away last night when we had checked in. But now, as the clicking of my wife's sandals echoed in the hallway, it seemed as though we were on an epic journey. Yesterday we had travelled two thousand miles from our home in the Midwest to Guatemala City. Now it felt like we were covering twice that distance in the span of a few minutes as we made our way to a hotel lobby in which sat a little eighteen-month-old girl who we knew would vastly alter the trajectory of our lives.

My wife reached the lobby first and let out a little gasp. Sitting on the lap of one of the mamas from the orphanage, her round face solemn, was Ellie.

Whitney took Ellie out of the caregiver's arms. This did not seem like a good idea to Ellie, who whirled around and looked with bewildered terror toward the mama who had given her up with so little persuasion. My wife continued to hold her, as tears began streaming down her own face. I tried to focus on my all-important job as videographer, but subsequent viewings of the video reveal my filming suffered from a case of the shakes.

Later, when I was able to pry her away from Whitney, I put Ellie on my lap and tried to look in her eyes. She quickly wrapped her arms tightly around me and pressed the side of her face against my chest. Pushing her away just a little from me, I looked at her face and tried to get her to smile. Her big, brown eyes briefly looked into mine, then quickly glanced down. She did not smile. She did not laugh. She whimpered slightly, then wrapped her arms around me again and buried her face in my chest.

This same scene would be repeated over and over again the next few days as we spent time in our hotel room awaiting our U.S. embassy appointment. Terrified of these new people and this strange room, Ellie spent most of her waking hours clinging to one of us. Try as we might, we could elicit no smile from her lips. Her brown eyes remained large, and she alternated between clinging to us and tucking her hands and arms safely out of sight.

The days blurred together. We were in our room. We were at our embassy appointment. We were on a plane. We were heading home.

When we arrived at the airport at home, the scene was chaotic. Our three older children met us there along with friends from church. Ellie continued to withdraw from the attention and noise. Our ride home in the minivan was quiet, and even though it was late, the big, beautiful eyes remained wide awake, quietly soaking in the scenes around her and slyly casting glances at her new siblings.

We walked into our home late that night and the older three children began to bring Ellie toys and show her around the house. Suddenly, as she interacted with her siblings, Ellie became an entirely different child. She was smiling at her big sister and even giggling at the antics of her older brothers. When we came into the room she would be sharing with her sister, all four kids piled onto the bed.

As they sat on the bed, Whitney quickly snapped a picture. It immediately became—and remains—one of my favorite photos. In the picture, on the far left of the frame is our oldest daughter Hannah. The boys, Austin and Noah, are laughing on the right side of the picture. Ellie, in the middle, is looking up at Hannah and smiling as we had never seen her smile. Tears welled up in my eyes as I saw the first glimpse of a new family.

Now that Ellie has been in our home over two years, she is a much-changed child. Challenges are still ahead of us, but the joys far outweigh the discouragements. There are so many ways that she brings delight to our lives. When I come home, she is the loudest of our four children to greet me. "Daddy!" she will shriek as she hurtles toward the front door. Wherever she is in the house, her little legs carry her quickly to her daddy. She is a great hugger—the little arms that once embraced me in fear now embrace me with joy. Her sheer enthusiasm for life is unsurpassed by anyone else I know.

But—and here is the crucial point—we did not embark on the journey of adoption so that I could hear a little girl who used to be an orphan cry, "Daddy!" We did not invest our time and resources just so we could experience the blessing of having a fourth child. We did not ask our friends and families to partner with us in the journey of adoption so that our table would have a sixth place setting. We believe that, as wonderful as all those things are, God has a grander reason for our adoption.

In this chapter, I would like us to do three things as we begin to discern that grand scheme. First, I want us to consider ways in which a Christian's care for orphans is not unique. Second, I want us to consider the purpose of the life of the believer as described in Ephesians 1:3–14. Finally, I hope to apply this purpose of life to orphan care, helping us understand what is unique about a Christian's care for the fatherless.

What Is *Not* Unique About Christian Orphan Care

When we adopted Ellie, we stayed at a hotel that was right next to the U.S. embassy. There were about five other families staying at the same hotel, all of whom were adopting children. When we went to our embassy appointment, about twenty more families were there with the children they wished to bring back to the States.

As we talked with some of the families who were adopting, we encountered people from diverse walks of life. Some were from the Northeast, some from the Southwest, some were old, some were young, some were married, and some were single. Each had a desire to welcome a new child into their home. I am confident that they all intended to love that child and provide him or her with the necessities of life: food, clothing, shelter, and a place to belong.

During the year that we received our referral, almost five thousand children were adopted from Guatemala by U.S. citizens. Overall, there were nearly twenty thousand adoptions in the United States that year. My point is that caring for orphans is not a strictly Christian phenomenon. There is nothing unique to Christianity about providing for orphaned children. Every day, unbelievers care for orphans. They visit orphanages. They donate to UNICEF. Every day, unbelievers bring children into their homes. They provide for them, care for them, and love them as they commit to sacrificing themselves for the benefit of their children.

A church or an individual who wishes to care for the fatherless must understand that our purpose is not merely to meet physical and emotional needs. There are many secular agencies that provide care and nourishment for orphans, and if that were our only goal and motivation, then our time would be better spent supporting entities that already exist.

The Purpose of Life

Before examining what makes the Christian's care for the fatherless unique, let us observe the purpose of life from Scripture's perspective. The primary text I would like us to consider here is Ephesians 1:3–14. We will look more closely at Ephesians 1:5–7 in chapter 3, but I want to take a moment and look at an overview of this passage and several others and consider what may be a paradigm-shifting truth for many.

The Glorious Grace of God

In the book of Ephesians, Paul lays out in chapters 1 through 3 how God calls people into the community of faith. He begins chapter 1 with a monstrously magnificent sentence that comprises verses 3–14. In our English translations, this long sentence has been broken down into smaller sentences in order to help us understand it, but in the Greek language, the sentence begins in verse 3 and continues through verse 14. The theme of this run-on (and on and on) sentence is why God should be blessed:

> Blessed be the God and Father of our Lord Jesus Christ, who has blessed us in Christ with every spiritual blessing in the heavenly places, even as he chose us in him before the foundation of the world, that we should be holy and blameless before him. In love he predestined us for adoption as sons through Jesus Christ, according to the purpose of his will, to the praise of his glorious grace, with which he has blessed us in the Beloved. In him we have redemption through his blood, the forgiveness of our trespasses, according to the riches of his grace, which he lavished upon us, in all wisdom and insight making known to us the mystery of his will, according to his purpose, which he set forth in Christ as a plan for the fullness of time, to unite all things in him, things in heaven and things on earth. In him we have obtained an inheritance, having been predestined according to the purpose of him who works all things according to the counsel of his will, so that we who were the first to hope in Christ might be to the praise of his glory. In him you also, when you heard the word of truth, the gospel of your salvation, and believed in him, were sealed with the promised Holy Spirit, who is the guarantee of our inheritance until we acquire possession of it, to the praise of his glory (Eph. 1:3–14).

Let me offer just a few observations about this text regarding who gives grace, who receives grace, and why grace is given.

God is the source of grace. God is the source of the lavish grace we have received. In the sentence, Paul gives four reasons that God should be blessed: He predestined us for adoption into his family (vv. 4–6); he redeemed us through the blood of Christ (vv. 9–10); he provided us with an inheritance (vv. 11–12); and, finally, he sealed us with the Holy Spirit (vv. 13–14).[1] As the primary agent in the sentence, God is the source of all good things. The only appropriate response, in Paul's mind, is to respond by blessing him!

We receive grace. God is the source of grace and we are the recipients of it. God predestines us. God redeems us. God provides an inheritance for us. It is not hard to see here the reasons Paul would call upon his audience to erupt in praise to God. In fact, how appropriate that the theme of such a long sentence is why God should be blessed. It is as if Paul is so carried away by the beauty of God's grace, he cannot bring himself to stop the sentence describing it!

As I sometimes hurriedly read over verses like Ephesians 1:3–14, I am reminded of present-opening time in the Bennett household. We have five rules for present opening with our children: (1) Open present. (2) If you already own what has been given to you, do not voluntarily disclose that information. (3) If the present is similar to an item that you requested but not exactly like what you wanted, do not under any circumstances mention that either. (4) Look the person who gave you the gift in the eye and express your undying and genuine gratitude for their gift. (5) Begin to open your next gift.

Unfortunately, it seems that my children sometimes have the tendency to go from step 1 to step 5 instantly, only taking a momentary pause to break rules 2 and 3 when applicable. At times, they have unfortunately given the impression that they do not truly appreciate what has just been given to them.

Let us be careful, then, not to skirt over these verses like an ungrateful child at a birthday party. May it never be said of us that we were careless in our gratitude to God for his matchless gifts! As Paul lays out the theological truths here, the response of the believer should be to meditate on the reality of these verses and apply them as Paul intended. The result of these truths should be that we bless God.

God's graciousness magnifies his glorious grace. Third, God is the agent of grace, we are the recipients of grace, and—here is the crucial

---

1. I have chosen to outline the sentence in terms of the major thematic reasons God should be blessed. Others rightly see a Trinitarian structure to the passage. Hoehner (*Ephesians: An Exegetical Commentary*, 174–245) observes the following outline: God's Election for Himself (vv. 4–6); God's Redemption in Christ (vv. 7–12); and, finally, God's Seal with the Spirit (vv. 13–14).

part—the purpose of all that he does is to magnify his glorious grace. Let me say this in a different way for greater clarity and emphasis: God's ultimate purpose in saving you is not your redemption but his glory! Fortunately, the two are not mutually exclusive. The former is a means to the latter.

A mother holds her adopted baby in her arms for the first time and experiences profound joy. Imagine you were to try and analyze why she was so happy at that moment. You ask her: "Has the child done something for you? Did he promise to someday pay you back for all of that money you shelled out to bring him home? Is he going to get back some of your attorney's fees?"

"Of course not," she replies. "I am filled with joy because he is my son."

And then you look at the baby, and you see that he too seems pretty happy. He coos and holds his new mother's finger and giggles as she uses the index finger on her other hand to tickle a spot on his neck. Her smile grows wider. "Why are you more happy?" you ask the mother. "How does his happiness make you happy? Shouldn't you just focus on your own happiness instead of his as well?"

"Of course not," she replies again. "My joy is increased as he finds delight in me. Our joys are not incompatible with one another."

God's focus on his glory does not mean that our joy decreases. Instead, his attention to our salvation brings us joy and increases his glory. Look again at these verses and see how his focus on his glory and the benefit we derive from his care of us intermingle. God planned our salvation from before the foundation of the world so that he would be praised for "his glorious grace" (v. 6). He redeemed us through Christ as part of an overreaching plan to "unite all things in him" (v. 10). Those who were the first to hope in Christ in the first century were "to the praise of his glory" (v. 12). He gave us an inheritance, and our reception of it will cause God's glory to be praised (v. 14).

Do you see the common theme? Throughout this passage, God's grace is what is exalted. Our adoption, our redemption, the gift of the Holy Spirit, our promised inheritance—these all are mentioned within the context of the glory God receives.

Be careful! While the temptation may be to focus on the benefits to humanity in these verses, a reading that ends with those benefits is superficial. The text forces us to come to this conclusion: God's ultimate purpose in bringing about our salvation is his own glory. Salvation is ultimately for God's glory and benefit, not our own. We exist to glorify God.

When we say that we exist to glorify God, what exactly does that mean? To glorify God does not mean that I add to God's value. God is infinitely glorious no matter what I do, and there is no way I can increase his glory. To glorify God is to reflect and proclaim his beauty. To glorify God is to worship him and display his value to others.

When Whitney and I decided to buy a vehicle several years ago, we started by looking at minivans for sale on the internet. What we found is that those who were trying to sell their minivans were "glorifying" them. The descriptions of the vehicles highlighted their best features. The pictures displayed the minivans in pleasant locales. All of them were neat and clean. Everything was designed to make the product look as good as possible.

Similarly, we are designed by God to live in such a way that we are walking advertisements for what a wonderful God he is. Nothing in our life should detract from his glory—everything should magnify it. Our task is infinitely easier than the task of the online car salesman for there are no flaws with God that we need to mask. Everything we do should demonstrate his infinite worth.

A Startling Truth

Some may understandably find this biblical truth confusing or unsettling. They may wonder if when we claim that God is passionate for himself above all others we are inadvertently accusing God of being sinfully selfish. I would suggest that, on the contrary, we are saying that God's value system is perfect. He rightly places the ultimate value on that which is of infinite worth—himself.

Imagine a diamond appraiser who was given a rare diamond and asked to calculate its worth. What would you think of his abilities if he assessed this priceless gem as worthless? Or suppose your city's real estate assessor estimated the value of your home to be ten times its real worth. If you were forced to pay exorbitantly high taxes because of his ineptitude, how highly would you rate his job performance? In both situations, these individuals would be wrong in their assessments and would rightly be considered to have done their jobs poorly.

God is never wrong in his assessment of worth. He is perfectly wise and able to assess the value of all things. God knows that his worth is infinitely superior to everyone else's. Nothing else in the entire universe has a fraction of his value. It would be wrong for him to value anything more than himself.

Now, consider the implications for fatherless children. If God's greatest passion is for his glory, does that mean God's love for little children is lessened? No! God's love for children is greater because he rightly prioritizes his own glory. If he valued anything more than himself, he would be elevating a creature above the Creator. God rightly places value on his own glory and lovingly calls us to do the same. He pursues what is best for us as he pursues his own glory.

So, of course God loves children! Scripture—and children's songs—correctly tell us that God loves the little children: red, brown, yellow, black, and white. All are precious in his sight! But—and again this should be considered as we will be looking at what makes a Christian adoption unique— God's love for children is not ultimate in his affections. His own glory is. God is more far more valuable than even precious children.

There are many places where the biblical truth that God's greatest passion is for his own glory is developed in greater detail, but consider just a few scriptural examples.[2] God delivered his people from Egypt "that he might make known his mighty power" (Ps. 106:7–8; cf. Exod. 14:4, 17–18). He forgives sins not on the basis of how wonderful the people are but "according to the greatness of [his] steadfast love" (Num. 14:13–19). God, through the prophet Isaiah, reveals how our very existence serves as a testimony to his glory: "everyone who is called by my name, *whom I created for my glory*, whom I formed and made" (Isa. 43:7; emphasis added).

The impact on our lives should be profound. There is no corner of our life that we can point to and tell God "hands off." He stands sovereign and authoritative over all realms. It is to his glory and our joy that we engage in all ministries, including orphan care. It is therefore incumbent upon us to carefully consider how he is to be glorified in this ministry of caring for children without parents.

God's plan to glorify his name has not reached its culmination yet. There are places in the world where his name is still not proclaimed. There are necks that still stiffen in rebellion to him. But God is patient, and his plan will reach its fulfillment. Habakkuk, ministering in the dark days of Judah's rebellion, looks not just to the day of her impending judgment but beyond that day to a time when "the earth will be filled with the knowledge of the glory of the Lord as the waters cover the sea" (Hab. 2:14).

Here is the purpose of our lives. We have been created for God's glory and the whole of human—indeed, universal—history is headed toward its climax with the full revelation of the glory of God. The heart of the child of God yearns for God's name to be exalted in all things.

What *Is* Unique About Christian Orphan Care

The success of the orphan ministry in your life or in your church's life hinges upon rightly understanding this purpose of life and seeing how an orphan care ministry fits into that framework.

I encourage you to think very carefully about why you want to be

---

2. John Piper's *Let the Nations Be Glad* was instrumental in helping me understand the biblical truths regarding the glory of God and the purpose of man.

involved in caring for orphans. We must scrutinize our motives and identify wrong reasons that might compel us to care for a child. Ultimately, what makes a Christian orphan ministry unique is its focus on the glory of God. No unbeliever approaches an orphanage with the thought of how God will be glorified in that place. No unbeliever cares for an orphan by praying that the worship of God would someday burst forth from the lips of that child.

If your employer told you that instead of cash bonuses this year, the company will be giving out free health club memberships to the most productive employees, your reaction would be commensurate with the value you place upon a health club membership. If you have no desire for such a membership, the carrot has little incentive for you. In fact, you may find it so unappealing that it serves as a disincentive. Similarly, the idea of an inheritance from the Lord can truly motivate only those who value him and his inheritance. Future rewards motivate us only to the degree we are convinced of the value and glory of our heavenly Father and his inheritance.

All proper motivation flows from an all-consuming passion for God's glory. People who are in love with the Lord will be motivated as they think about the eternal reward their heavenly Father has promised. Consider the exhortation and motivation of Colossians 3:23–24: "Whatever you do, work heartily, as for the Lord and not for men, knowing that from the Lord you will receive the inheritance as your reward. You are serving the Lord Christ." Paul's point is that we should get excited as we consider our reward. The inheritance of God seems a paltry compensation for the person who is not passionate about God. For those who are filled with an all-consuming passion for his glory, no reward could be greater!

SMALL GROUP DISCUSSION GUIDE[3]

FELLOWSHIP AND PRAYER
This time provides the opportunity to develop relationships and share ongoing prayer concerns.

STARTER QUESTIONS
1. What are some of your goals in going through this study? What are some of the questions you have about orphan care ministry that you would like to make sure are covered?
2. Are there ways God has used you in the past to care for the orphan? How have you been encouraged by how he has used others?

---

3. See preface for suggestions regarding study groups.

3. What are some ways that you believe God might call you to care for the orphan in the future?

SCRIPTURE TO CONSIDER

1. Read through Ephesians 1:3–14. Write down several observations from the text and discuss what it teaches us concerning the purpose of our life. How well are you fulfilling your responsibility to bless God for his gracious provision of your salvation?
2. Read the following verses and note what they teach us about God's glory.
   • Isaiah 48:9–11
   • Matthew 5:16
   • 1 Peter 2:12

REVIEWING PRINCIPLES FROM THE CHAPTER

1. What are some ways that Christian orphan care is not unique?
2. Why do we exist? What is the purpose of our lives? What are some examples from Scripture of God's passion for his glory?
3. What are some ways that Christian orphan care is unique?

APPLICATION QUESTIONS

1. How does being a Christian change the manner in which we meet the physical needs of orphans? Or, to put it another way, how does understanding that the purpose of our lives is to glorify God impact our ministry to orphans?
2. How does shifting our ultimate focus from children to God help us serve children more effectively?
3. Do you have a desire to meet the needs of orphans? Why or why not? What motivates you, or would motivate you, to care for them?

2 Compassion, the Disenfranchised, and the Orphan

The images pouring in from Haiti after the earthquake struck Port-au-Prince on January 12, 2010 were hard to process. Bodies lined the streets. Survivors sat on curbs, with sunken eyes, each overwhelmed by a story of personal tragedy. Sometimes there was a rustle of activity. Sometimes no one did anything. Over the coming days and weeks, the number of estimated fatalities would be frequently revised until it was more than 200,000 souls.

We watched the scenes in horror, and Christ's church responded. As is true after any major disaster, large amounts of money were raised and resources were provided to help the people of Haiti. Orphan ministries across the United States were flooded with requests from Christians who wanted to help the children in Haitian orphanages and those children who may have been newly orphaned.

In some situations, however, the church is slower to respond. The United Nations World Food Programme estimates that one billion people do not have enough to eat—that is more than the populations of the United States, Canada, and the countries that make up the European Union combined. Every six seconds, a child dies of hunger and related causes. Eleven million children under five die each year in developing countries, and more than 60 percent of those deaths can be attributed to hunger and malnutrition. Lack of vitamin A kills a million infants a year.[1]

Amazingly, the cost of providing assistance for orphans and other vulnerable children is estimated to only be about thirty cents a day per child. Studies indicate that "religious" Americans are far more likely to give than any other sub-group,[2] but even their giving fails to reflect the urgency of

---

1. World Food Programme, "Hunger," http://www.wfp.org/hunger.
2. See Brooks's *Who Really Cares: The Surprising Truth About Compassionate Conservatism.* For example, he wrote: "Religious people are far more charitable than nonreligious people, I have never found a measurable way in which secularists are more charitable than religious people" (p. 34).

the need. While much of the world goes hungry, the church fails to respond with appropriate concern. More money is spent on diet programs than it would take to alleviate world hunger. In fact, more money is spent on feeding our pets than would be required to feed those who are hungry. Today, Americans will waste almost five times the amount of food that is provided in global aid.[3] We do not act as though we believe we have an obligation to proactively care for the impoverished in the world.

In the North American evangelical church, there is a growing awareness that we have not adequately focused on the needs of the destitute or the disenfranchised. To be disenfranchised means you do not possess the privileges and abilities enjoyed by the rest of a society. This awareness has manifested itself in different ways. Politically, it has meant that some American evangelicals—a group that traditionally votes conservatively—are reconsidering their allegiance to the Republican Party. *Newsweek* magazine termed this "An Evangelical Identity Crisis," and notes that many evangelicals are "going back to the Bible and embracing a wider-ranging agenda, one that emphasizes reaching out to the poor and disenfranchised."[4]

Unfortunately, this growing concern for the disenfranchised has caused some evangelicals to theologically redefine the church. One prominent pastor sent shockwaves through the evangelical community—perhaps unintentionally—when he radically redefined the term "evangelical" during an interview with the *Boston Globe*. "I embrace the term evangelical," Rob Bell remarked, "if by that we mean a belief that we together can actually work for change in the world, caring for the environment, extending to the poor generosity and kindness, a hopeful outlook. That's a beautiful sort of thing."[5]

But that is certainly not what I mean when I use the term "evangelical." This sentiment, while seemingly "beautiful," is at odds with the biblical and historical understanding of what it means to be evangelical. Bell's definition shifts the focus of the church from proclaiming Christ to fighting social ills. The essence of the church is changed from union with Christ through the gospel to a do-gooder social club.

There is a contemporary movement within the church whose adherents refer to themselves as "emergent" or, sometimes, "progressive evangelicals." Brian McLaren, a pastor and leading voice in the emergent

---

3. These statistics come from www.stopthehunger.com, a real-time statistics project (accessed November 20, 2010).
4. Miller, "An Evangelical Identity Crisis."
5. Paulson, "Rob Bell on Faith, Suffering, and Christians."

movement, is also trying to radically redefine the church. As the *Washington Post* put it, "McLaren . . . offers an evangelical vision that emphasizes tolerance and social justice. He contends that people can follow Jesus' way without becoming Christian. . . . [He] argues that Christians should be more concerned about creating a just 'Kingdom of God' on earth than about getting into heaven."[6] McLaren believes that some Christians see Christianity as an escape from the present world instead of a call to engage it. We should see Jesus "as entering the world to bring healing and hope for creation." Therefore, "we need to join him in incarnation, in entering into humanity's pain and suffering and oppression, and bringing God's amazing resources to bear."[7]

Before offering a critique of this position, let me first acknowledge that I believe every serious, Bible-believing Christian should consider the words of these progressives very carefully. There may indeed be a need for repentance on our part for not being more engaged in following the example of our Lord in caring for the poor.

Yet there is a real problem with their call to social action. It focuses on social change at the *expense* of the gospel instead of in *conjunction* with the gospel. Many progressive evangelicals have issued a call to action while simultaneously jettisoning the traditional, biblical understanding of the church. Their new church is not passionately grounded in the faith handed down by the apostles and prophets (e.g., Eph. 2:20).

Worship, not social activism, is the ultimate goal of the church. Justice flows from worship as surely as the melted snow causes the rivers to flow down the mountain in the spring. Defining the church primarily as an agent for social change fundamentally alters its purpose. Instead of social good flowing from the ultimate goal of the church that is worship, social good becomes the ultimate goal.

While Jesus' call was certainly a call to live like him, it was not separated from a doctrinal understanding of who he is. Indeed, he frequently rebuked the Pharisees for their faulty doctrine that caused their wrong understanding of him and prevented them from living as they ought (e.g., Mark 12:10–11).

In short, a ministry to the poor must be theologically grounded. We must fastidiously avoid a Faustian bargain of exchanging our theology for pragmatism, gaining the esteem of the world at the expense of our soul. The consequence of separating theology from practice is a call to compassion not rooted in a solid understanding of the character of God. This type

---

6. Murphy, "Evangelical Author Puts Progressive Spin on Traditional Faith."
7. Christianbook.com, "Interview with Brian McLaren."

of compassion that many are mistakenly calling us to is what I call "passion-less compassion."

The Problem of Passionless Compassion

With passionless compassion, concern for the disenfranchised is not motivated by a passion for the glory of the triune God. Instead, the good works of involvement in social issues—like caring for orphans—becomes an end in itself. Zeal for people, divorced from right doctrine concerning the God who calls one to care for them, will lead to no eternal benefit for ourselves or those we help.

In *When Helping Hurts: How to Alleviate Poverty Without Hurting the Poor and Yourself*, Steve Corbett and Brian Fikkert examine the largely unsuccessful efforts of developed countries to combat global poverty. In a chapter entitled, "McDevelopment: Over 2.5 Billion People Not Served," the authors lament our wasted efforts at caring for the impoverished:

> Despite an estimated $2.3 trillion in foreign aid dispensed from Western nations during the post–World War II era, more than 2.5 billion people, approximately 40 percent of the world's population, still live on less than two dollars per day. And the story in many North American communities is similar, with one initiative after another failing to meet its intended objectives. Indeed, forty-five years after President Johnson launched the War on Poverty, the poverty rate in America stubbornly hovers around 12 percent, decade after decade, year after year.[8]

The world does not need more people to feel sorry for the poor. The world desperately needs Christians whose lives have been transformed by a passion for God, which flows into a passion for others.

Elizabeth Styffe, the director of Saddleback's HIV/AIDS Initiative, was in Malawi when God overwhelmed her with compassion for the orphan. Standing in a cold, dark, and damp hut that was no bigger than four feet by six feet, she looked down at the three young children who lived there. The children's faces were expressionless, evidencing no emotion whatsoever. "They had the blankest faces I have ever seen. It was almost as though they weren't alive. There was no response. Absolutely no connection."[9]

---

8. Corbett and Fikkert, *When Helping Hurts*, 141–42.
9. Elizabeth Styffe, phone conversation with author, February 18, 2010.

Elizabeth is a person who is naturally outgoing and connects well with children. Her complete inability to engage these children unnerved her. She asked her interpreter where their mother was.

"They have no parents," was the reply.

"Who will put them to bed tonight? Who will feed them in the morning?" she asked.

"No one."

The children were part of a child-headed household. No one was responsible to provide food for them. No one tucked them in when they lay down on their mats at night and darkness engulfed them. There was no mother to cry out to. No adult to cling to when the night terrors came. Day after day and night after night, these three little children had to fend for themselves.

I don't know how to comprehend that awful reality. Neither did Elizabeth. She stood face to face not with three statistics but with three flesh-and-blood children who had no one to care for them. As the awful reality of their situation came crashing down on her, there was only one feasible response: heart-breaking, stomach-wrenching, life-altering compassion.

The argument of this chapter is that *true compassion for the needy is always fueled by a passion for God to be worshipped among them*. It could also be said that the reverse is true: genuine passion for God to be worshipped will always be manifested by a concern for the needy. We will consider this argument by focusing on three truths: (1) God has compassion for the disenfranchised; (2) God's people have compassion for the disenfranchised; and, finally, (3) true compassion is fueled by a passion for God to be worshipped.

God Has Compassion for the Disenfranchised

The word that is translated "compassion" in our English Bibles means "to be inwardly moved." It refers to the sensation one should have when one encounters someone in need. It is what welled up within Elizabeth as she looked into the vacant eyes of those three Malawi children in their hut and realized no one was there for them. To understand compassion, we must first realize we have the capacity to feel compassion because we serve a mighty and gracious God.

God Is a Compassionate God: Exodus 33:19

Compassion is one of the attributes of God that is often highlighted in Scripture when explaining God's relationship to humanity. His compassion toward us enables us to live and enter into fellowship with him. When God threatens the destruction of the Israelites following their worship of the golden calf, Moses pleads with God to remain with his people. Furthermore, he asks that God would demonstrate his presence with his people by showing his glory. It is an audacious request, but the Lord agrees. "I will make all my goodness pass before you and will proclaim before you my name 'The Lord.' And I will be gracious to whom I will be gracious, and will show mercy on whom I will show mercy" (Exod. 33:19).

This compassion that God has for us is not based upon our worth, nor is it part of a quid-pro-quo arrangement. God's compassion is internally motivated and causes him to act in our interest. I will affirm again in this chapter that his ultimate motivation is for his glory, but we should not allow that truth to compromise another great biblical truth: God is a gracious and compassionate God *and that compassion benefits us.* He spares sinners and provides for their needs when they deserve destruction.

Groups That Receive God's Special Compassion: Exodus 22:21–27

There are times when my attention is drawn to one of my children in particular based upon a need that the child has at a given time. For example, my daughter may need help writing a paper or my son may need a good wrestling. Whatever the reason, based upon the need, I focus on that child in a unique way. As we examine Scripture on the subject of God's compassion, we notice four groups that draw God's special attention based upon their unique needs.

Four disenfranchised groups in Scripture. The groups that are frequently cited in Scripture as being particularly needy are the foreigner, the widow, the orphan, and the poor. These groups are mentioned together in Exodus 22. God instructs his people:

> You shall not wrong a sojourner or oppress him, for you were sojourners in the land of Egypt. You shall not mistreat any widow or fatherless child. If you do mistreat them, and they cry out to me, I will surely hear their cry, and my wrath will burn, and I will kill you with the sword, and your wives shall become widows and your children fatherless.
>
> If you lend money to any of my people with you who is poor, you shall not be like a moneylender to him, and you shall not exact interest from him. If ever you take your neighbor's cloak in pledge, you shall return it to him before the sun goes down, for that is his only covering, and it is his cloak for his body; in what else shall he sleep? And if he cries to me, I will hear, for I am compassionate. (Exod. 22:21–27)

The first group mentioned, foreigners (v. 21), often lack the skills and connections necessary to survive in a community. The second and third groups, widows and orphans (vv. 22–24), in many cultures are deprived of family members who could care for them. On their own, they lack the ability to provide themselves. The fourth group, the poor (vv. 25–27), can easily be exploited by those who have the resources they lack. God's message to his people is clear: he is a fierce advocate of the defenseless. When they cry to him, he will hear, for he is compassionate" (v. 27).

God is aware of the disenfranchised. God is mindful of the plight of these four groups. He notices them and observes how others care for them. As we take into account the observations made in Scripture concerning the character of God and his concern for the disenfranchised, it becomes clear that God is an active defender of the needy.

> O LORD, you hear the desire of the afflicted; you will strengthen their heart; you will incline your ear to do justice to the fatherless and the oppressed, so that man who is of the earth may strike terror no more. (Ps. 10:17–18)

> Father of the fatherless and protector of widows is God in his holy habitation. (Ps. 68:5)

> For he delivers the needy when he calls, the poor and him who has no helper. He has pity on the weak and the needy, and saves the lives of the needy. From oppression and violence he redeems their life, and precious is their blood in his sight. Long may he live; may gold of Sheba be given to him! May prayer be made for him continually, and blessings invoked for him all the day! (Ps. 72:12–15)

> Who is like the LORD our God, who is seated on high, who looks far down on the heavens and the earth? He raises the poor from the dust and lifts the needy from the ash heap. (Ps. 113:5–7)

> The LORD watches over the sojourners; he upholds the widow and the fatherless, but the way of the wicked he brings to ruin. (Ps. 146:9)

> In you the orphan finds mercy. (Hos. 14:3b)

It is impossible to give these texts a fair reading without coming to the conclusion that God has a special care for those who are the neediest in a society. These four groups that may be forgotten by some are nevertheless remembered by a Sovereign God.

The dangerous place between God and the disenfranchised. It seemed like a good idea at the time. I needed to burn up some tree limbs and I needed to get rid of some old gasoline. I thought that I could combine the two projects and save a little time. After starting the fire on one side of the brush pile, I sloshed some gasoline on the other. Flames quickly engulfed the area where I had applied the flammable liquid. I continued doing this, splashing a small amount of gasoline on an area of the brush pile where the flames seemed to be subsiding, amazed at how such a small quantity of fuel could result in such a large amount of fire.

You can imagine my surprise when I looked down and saw that the gas can I was holding was on fire. As I looked down at the flaming can, I experientially realized what a dangerous thing I had been doing. I threw the can into the fire and ran. In my mind's eye, I pictured the can exploding behind me and my adrenaline-powered jump to safety, like in the movies.

Fortunately for me, those who design gas cans apparently do so thinking, "What is the dumbest thing someone could do with this can?" and plan accordingly. It did not explode but burned like a fire-spouting candle until the fuel was extinguished.

There is something even more foolish than holding onto a flaming gas can, and that is standing between God and the orphan. You see, God's care for the orphan is not passive. The following passages have an overriding theme: God will care for the helpless and deal with those who take advantage of or neglect them!

He executes justice for the fatherless and the widow, and loves the sojourner, giving him food and clothing. Love the sojourner, therefore, for you were sojourners in the land of Egypt. (Deut. 10:18–19)

You shall not pervert the justice due to the sojourner or to the fatherless, or take a widow's garment in pledge, but you shall remember that you were a slave in Egypt and the Lord your God redeemed you from there; therefore I command you to do this. When you reap your harvest in your field and forget a sheaf in the field, you shall not go back to get it. It shall be for the sojourner, the fatherless, and the widow, that the Lord your God may bless you in all the work of your hands." (Deut. 24:17–19)

Cursed be anyone who perverts the justice due to the sojourner, the fatherless, and the widow. (Deut. 27:19a)

Do not move an ancient landmark or enter the fields of the fatherless, for their Redeemer is strong; he will plead their cause against you. (Prov. 23:10–11)

Then I will draw near to you for judgment. I will be a swift witness against … those who oppress the hired worker in his wages, the widow and the fatherless, against those who thrust aside the sojourner, and do not fear me, says the LORD of hosts. (Mal. 3:5)

From these passages, I arrive at the very sobering conclusion that it is a dangerous thing to stand between God and the needy. I do not want to get in the way of God's provision for the disenfranchised either through intentional oppression or unintentional neglect.

The Essence of God's Compassion: Isaiah 61:1–3

It is essential that we understand why God bestows his compassion on these groups of people. In Isaiah 61:1–3, we gain an important insight into what motivates his compassion for the needy.

The Spirit of the Lord GOD is upon me, because the LORD has anointed me to bring good news to the poor; he has sent me to bind up the brokenhearted, to proclaim liberty to the captives, and the opening of the prison to those who are bound; to proclaim the year of the LORD's favor, and the day of vengeance of our God; to comfort all who mourn; to grant to those who mourn in Zion—to give them a beautiful headdress instead of ashes, the oil of gladness instead of mourning, the garment of praise instead of a faint spirit; that they may be called oaks of righteousness, the planting of the LORD, that he may be glorified.

Isaiah proclaims that there is good news being proclaimed to the disenfranchised. These people are "poor," "brokenhearted," "captives," and "bound." Based upon the New Testament's usage of Isaiah 61, we see that these people are poor in both a physical and a spiritual sense.[10] The good

---

10. In commenting on Jesus' use of Isaiah 61 in Luke 4, Darrell Bock wrote: "Jesus' portrayal as light and liberator to the poor, captive, and blind is a crucial point in the passage and has been the subject of much discussion, even

news is that there is deliverance at hand and their relationship with God will be restored. The best news, and the climax of the passage, is that they will become "oaks of righteousness" and therefore God will be glorified. God's compassion results in God's glory.

The motivation behind God's compassion is his glory. God's compassion ends with his glory! This simply confirms the truth we considered in the previous chapter. All God does is ultimately for his glory. To rightly understand compassion, we must understand its proper end—the magnification of our heavenly Father.

The Problem with Passionless Compassion

The problem with passionless compassion is that it sees the means—compassion—as an end. It focuses on good deeds without first focusing on the worship that should motivate the believer to engage in them. Compassion is a means to an end and not the end itself.

My children enjoy Amelia Bedelia books. Amelia Bedelia is a lovable but scatterbrained maid who struggles to accomplish even the simplest tasks. When her employers, Mr. and Mrs. Rogers, give her instructions, she takes the words literally, and in the process, she fails to do what they have actually asked her to do. When they instruct her to "draw the drapes," Amelia Bedelia sits down and draws a picture of the drapes; when she is told to "measure two cups of rice," she pours out two cups of rice, pulls out a tape measure and measures them, then pours the rice back into the box. Technically, she does what she is told to do, but she does so without understanding the context and purpose for which the instruction is given.[11]

Evangelicals are sometimes compassionate in an Amelia Bedelia type of way. While we are literally doing what we have been told to do, our actions show we lack the theological understanding to know what God is really concerned about. We fall so far short of what he truly wishes us to do

spawning a theology—liberation theology—focused around passages like Luke 4. . . . The images of Luke 4 cannot be treated as individual promises and broken up from each other, so that one isolates social elements from spiritual elements. The imagery operates as a unit, picturing the totality of Jesus' deliverance. All the images have to do with the comprehensiveness of Jesus' message and the hope that he offers people" (*Luke*, 400). Joel Green also argues against interpretations that define the term *poor* in a purely spiritual or a purely economic sense and maintains that the poor should be seen in a "holistic sense" (*The Gospel of Luke*, 210–213).

11. Parish, *Amelia Bedelia*.

that our actions are nonsensical. Compassion must be fueled by passion for God or it is not compassion at all.

God's People Have Compassion for the Disenfranchised

Every January, our church observes "Sanctity of Life Sunday," or, as I call it, "Tissue Sunday." On this day we place a special emphasis on the orphan ministry. As we share testimonies regarding how God has been at work in the lives of families in the church, it is not unusual to see people wiping away some tears. Our hearts are overwhelmed with emotion as we consider not only the current provision for these children but also the effect this ministry will have into eternity. As I tell Whitney when she and her friends are reading one another's blogs, getting people who love children to become emotional about caring for orphans is like asking a pastor to stand up and say a few words. The problem is not a lack of enthusiasm but perhaps overeagerness.

And that is good. We are not nihilists who have become so cynical to the harsh realities of this world that we no longer feel pain. God has given us emotions, and they can sometimes help us rightly respond to the truth. Our hearts should be soft enough to feel sorrow and ache as we wrestle with life here under the sun. God is a compassionate God and compassion is a tool he uses to motivate his people to respond to the painful world in which we shed our tears.

That being said, I urge caution when utilizing emotional videos or stories in your church. Emotions alone are not enough to sustain interest in a ministry or to properly motivate people to serve for God's glory. By themselves, emotions do not properly prepare us for ministry. We must not rely upon moving stories alone to compel people to be involved in any ministry.

When compassion springs from a heart that does not love the Lord or have an understanding of his glory, it is not godly compassion. Worldly compassion comes from a heart that is commendably aware of and sensitive to the needs of others. The heart in which worldly compassion originates, however, is permeated with motives that are not God-glorifying. Pride in our social consciousness or guilt over our abundant material possessions are often at the root of worldly compassion.

Worldly compassion is sometimes displayed by people who desire others to help meet a need they have identified. In Jane Austen's *Mansfield Park*, young Fanny Price is cared for by her aunt and uncle at the behest of another aunt, Mrs. Norris. Mrs. Norris has no desire to participate in the care of Fanny but instead enjoys being generous with her relatives' possessions. "As far as walking, talking, and contriving reached, she was thoroughly benevolent, and nobody knew better how to dictate liberality to others; but her love of money was equal to her love of directing, and she knew quite as well how to save her own as to spend that of her friends."[12]

Worldly compassion is ultimately unproductive in meeting the true needs of the orphan. It may meet physical needs, but it is abysmally short-sighted when it comes to meeting long-term spiritual needs. Worldly compassion does not compel a person to action that has an eternal benefit.

The Necessity of Biblical Compassion in the Life of the Believer: Luke 10:25–37

My first seminary class was an introduction to missions, taught by Dr. Mark Young, who now serves as the president of Denver Theological Seminary. In our initial session, Dr. Young taught on Luke 10:25–37, where we find the parable of the Good Samaritan. A lawyer had also put Jesus to a test:

> "Teacher, what shall I do to inherit eternal life?" He said to him, "What is written in the Law? How do you read it?" And he answered, "You shall love the Lord your God with all your heart and with all your soul and with all your strength and with all your mind, and your neighbor as yourself." And he said to him, "You have answered correctly; do this, and you will live." But he, desiring to justify himself, said to Jesus, "And who is my neighbor?" (vv. 25–27)

Engaging in a rabbinic dialogue, this lawyer asks Jesus a question, and Jesus turns the question back on him. The lawyer asserts that love of God and love of neighbor are essential for the one who would claim eternal life. Jesus concurs. But the lawyer is a little unsettled. He knows his love for others is deficient, and he also attempts to engage Jesus again with one of the most profound questions in all of Scripture for the one who wishes to have a biblical understanding of caring for the fatherless: "And who is my neighbor?"

The story of the Good Samaritan's decision to help the man who fell among robbers is Jesus' reply to this question. Jesus concludes his story with a question. "Which of these three, do you think, proved to be a neighbor to

---

12. Austen, 428.

the man who fell among the robbers?' He said, 'The one who showed him mercy.' And Jesus said to him, "You go, and do likewise" (vv. 36–37).

Dr. Young drew three key truths out of this parable that were life altering for me: (1) love of God and love of neighbor are essential characteristics of one who has eternal life; (2) we must have an unlimited concept of who our neighbor is; and (3) compassion compels us to action.

There must be a stirring in our hearts when we as believers are confronted with a need. This compassion, however, causes us not only to feel but to do for the glory of God. This differentiates it from worldly compassion or mere emotionalism. Biblical compassion is not idle.

Compassion and the Orphan

As we saw earlier, God has a special concern for the poor, the foreigner, and the widow and orphan. This means that *we as believers should have a love for our neighbor the orphan that compels us to action.* There is no other alternative. We do not have the prerogative to turn a blind eye to the plight of the fatherless. We cannot be like the priest or Levite of Jesus' parable who walk on by the orphan in need. We see the need, and our hearts yearn for God to be glorified, and we are compelled by compassion to action.

Sharron, a family friend who is a nurse, went to Uganda to visit an orphanage. The trip was both physically and emotionally draining. As Sharron left the place where she had been ministering, she wrote on her blog, "Our hearts are shattered. . . . " She was broken as she cared for these little ones, but compassion compelled her. "I need Africa," she wrote, "more than Africa needs me." Such is the condition of the heart of the believer: ever-aching, yet continuing to feel and love and care because of compassion.

As she cared for one child in particular, Sharron and her husband were moved by compassion to begin the process of adopting him. The child who touched their hearts has serious health problems. She and her husband have a complicated life already. What compelled them to undertake such a difficult ministry? In a word—compassion.

Perhaps you have been moved by compassion by some event in your life. You saw children in an orphanage, and your heart broke as you pleaded with God to help you meet their needs no matter what the cost. You were moved by compassion as you have heard the story of a couple who is adopting, and you decided to forgo the vacation you had been saving for and support that couple instead. Perhaps you are being moved by compassion even now as you think about the souls of little children who are in need of physical and spiritual aid. Compassion is an essential attribute of the believer whose soul has been transformed by the gospel.

True Compassion Is Fueled by a Passion for God to Be Worshipped

The argument of this chapter is that true compassion for the needy must be fueled by a passion for God to be worshipped among them and—conversely—that passion for the worship of God will manifest itself in care for the needy.

The Compassion of Christ

In Christ's ministry, his compassion is fueled by a desire for God to be worshipped. His gospel message and compassion are linked in passages like Matthew 9:35–38:

> And Jesus went throughout all the cities and villages, teaching in their synagogues and proclaiming the gospel of the kingdom and healing every disease and every affliction. When he saw the crowds, he had compassion for them, because they were harassed and helpless, like sheep without a shepherd. Then he said to his disciples, "The harvest is plentiful, but the laborers are few; therefore pray earnestly to the Lord of the harvest to send out laborers into his harvest."

The good news of the kingdom includes relief from oppression, both spiritual and physical (see, e.g., Matt. 4:16, 23; 11:28–29). The first effects of the kingdom are felt as forgiveness and healing take place through Jesus' ministry, but central to his message is a call to enter the kingdom through repentance (4:17).

In Matthew 9, however, the people do not come to Jesus because of his message of repentance. They are not so overwhelmed by their spiritual need that they come to Jesus. Their response is driven by baser motives. Nevertheless, as Jesus sees them come to him, he feels compassion. Even knowing their innermost thoughts and their lack of repentance, Jesus feels compassion for sinners. He is aware of the spiritual oppression under which the people are laboring, and he desires to see them freed.

Jesus responds to this need by calling his disciples to pray for the harvest. The good news is that the harvest is plentiful—there are many needy people. The bad news is that the workers are few. Only a few are compassionate and respond to the physical and spiritual needs of the people. The response should be to pray that God does what it takes to mobilize his army. Passionate prayer, Jesus is saying, precedes God's provision.

God loves for people to be saved, and that is Jesus' desire here as well. Let's bring in more workers, he says, so that these lost ones can experience the transformation of the gospel for the glory of God! The psalmist declares that God is the one who "delivers the needy when he calls, the poor and him who has no helper. He has pity on the weak and the needy, and saves the lives of the needy. From oppression and violence he redeems their life, and precious is their blood in his sight. Long may he live; may gold of Sheba be given to him! May prayer be made for him continually, and blessings invoked for him all the day!" (Ps. 72:12–15). And, as God proclaims in Malachi 1:11, "For from the rising of the sun to its setting my name will be great among the nations, and in every place incense will be offered to my name, and a pure offering. For my name will be great among the nations, says the LORD of hosts." God will be worshipped—from the lips of the lowliest will come songs of praise.

True Compassion for the Orphan

Our primary desire for orphans is to see them burst forth in worship of God. This passion will inevitably flow into a desire to meet their physical needs as well. If we do not have a compassion for the needy, it is possible that our passion is not for the true God but for an idolatrous substitute. True compassion for the needy is always fueled by a passion for God to be worshipped among them—and a passion for God always manifests itself in compassion for others. May God give us the grace to care for the needy, fueled by a passion for God to be worshipped among them!

SMALL GROUP DISCUSSION GUIDE

FELLOWSHIP AND PRAYER

STARTER QUESTIONS

1. Can you think of a particular instance in which you were moved by compassion to take action?
2. Can you think of a time when someone showed compassion to you? How did it affect your life?

SCRIPTURE TO CONSIDER

1. Read the following verses and note what they teach us about God's passion for the disenfranchised.
   - Proverbs 23:10–11
   - Malachi 3:5
   - James 5:4

2. Read the following verses from the Gospels and note what they teach us about Jesus' compassion.
   - Matthew 9:35–38
   - Mark 6:30–44
   - Luke 7:11–17

REVIEWING PRINCIPLES FROM THE CHAPTER

1. What are some ways that the church has divorced theology from its concern for the disenfranchised?
2. What is meant by the phrase "passionless compassion"? Why is it so dangerous?
3. What are the special groups that receive special attention from God in Scripture? How have the needs of each of those groups changed? How have they remained the same? How is your church caring for each of these groups? As you consider ministry in your cultural context, what is unique about the needs of orphans compared with the other groups?
4. Why is God compassionate? Why does he show special compassion for some?
5. In the chapter it was claimed that true compassion for the needy is always fueled by a passion for God to be worshipped among them, and that a passion for God always manifests itself in compassion for others. Do you agree with this statement? How does your care for orphans currently reflect the passion you have for God? How can you discern if your passion for God is idolatrous?
6. Why is compassion an essential characteristic of the believer?
7. What is our ultimate desire for the orphan?

APPLICATION QUESTIONS

1. Who are the disenfranchised people in your life?
2. How has your passion for God influenced your compassion for the needy?
3. Below are some statistics from UNICEF regarding the needs of orphans. As you read through them, consider what the biblical response is to these statistics.

Water, Sanitation, and Hygiene[13]
- In the developing world, 60 million children are born each year into households without proper sanitation facilities.

---

13. UNICEF, "Water, Sanitation and Hygiene."

• More than 5,000 children die every day of diarrheal diseases, 88 percent of which are caused by lack of sanitary condition.

Child Protection[14]
• In sub-Saharan Africa, 69 million children are engaged in child labor.
• Worldwide, 250,000 children are involved in armed conflicts in various capacities such as combatants or spies, or forced to perform sexual services.
• Approximately 1.2 million children are trafficked worldwide every year, a business that generates approximately $9.5 billion annually.
• Eight million boys and girls live in institutional care, where they are far more likely to be engaged in violent acts or abused sexually.

Child Survival and Development[15]
• One child under five dies every three seconds (approximately 25,000 daily) from primarily preventable causes.
• An infant in a developing country is ten times more likely to die than a newborn in an industrialized country.

HIV and AIDS[16]
• In 2007, it was estimated that about 2.1 million children under fifteen were living with HIV.
• Of all children with HIV, 90 percent live in sub-Saharan Africa.
• There are 12.1 million children in sub-Saharan Africa who have been orphaned by AIDS.

4. What is your plan to respond to the needs of your neighbor the orphan?
5. Are we required to meet every need that we see? How do we determine what needs to meet?
6. Why is an adoption ministry alone not sufficient to meet the biblical injunction to care for the fatherless?

---

14. UNICEF, "Child Protection."
15. UNICEF, "Child Survival and Development."
16. UNICEF, "HIV and AIDS."

3 God's Glorious Grace *and* Orphan Care

Robert and Grace have seven children. Three are their biological children, three of them were adopted through the foster system, and one was adopted from Guatemala. Though this may not raise eyebrows in the adoption circles in which you run, there is a question that comes to the mind of many in our culture when they hear that someone has seven children: *Why?!* What would possess a rational couple to take upon themselves the responsibility to provide for so many children? What about their retirement plans? What about paying college tuition? What about their "me time"?

I have learned a lot about the joy and difficulty of being obedient to God through selfless service by watching Robert and Grace. There are three things from their story that are relevant to the theme of this chapter. First, Robert and Grace made a plan to care for orphans. Children did not show up one morning on their doorstep with all the necessary paperwork filled out. It was a lengthy process to formulate a plan to fulfill God's call.

Second, Robert and Grace worked to provide what was necessary to care for orphans. Not only did they make plans but they then invested emotionally, spiritually, and financially to bring those plans to fruition. I had the privilege of being in the courtroom when the adoption of two of their children was finalized. Witnessing the last leg of their adoption journey, my eyes were moist with tears as a judge formally recognized what had already taken place in the hearts of Robert, Grace, and their children. Years of planning and work reached fulfillment as Brian and Mandy were declared part of Robert and Grace's family.

Finally, Robert and Grace took pleasure in the fruit of their labors. While there are struggles, which is always true in a parent-child relationship, Robert and Grace love their children. They take great delight in them, even though they feel pain as they consider the tragic circumstances that made those children a part of their family. I enjoy being in their loud and happy home.

The planning, the provision for care, and the pleasure in the ministry are all demonstrations of grace on the part of our friends. You cannot help but be excited as you see the effects of grace in their life. When I once asked Robert and Grace how they could be so gracious to others, they paused, almost as if they thought the question was a little silly. They told me that God's grace toward them is the boundless reserve from which they draw their ability to show grace to others.

The Glorious Grace of God Proclaimed by His Care for Orphans

God cares for the spiritually needy just as he cares for those who have physical needs. Ephesians reveals that we were dead in our sins and living wasted, futile lives (2:1–3; 4:17–18). In order to rescue us from this state in which we found ourselves, God adopted us.

We already considered the great theme of the glory of God in Ephesians 1:3–14. As we look more closely at verses 5 and 6, we see that it is God's grace specifically that causes him to be glorified as he cares for the spiritual orphan: "he predestined us for adoption as sons through Jesus Christ, according to the purpose of his will, to the praise of his glorious grace, with which he has blessed us in the Beloved."

God's adoption of us is such an incredible act that all who ponder it should praise him for his graciousness. In this chapter, I want us to look at three ways that God's adoption of us results in the praise of his grace. Then, we will discuss how we should respond to such lavish grace.

God's Glorious Grace in Our Adoption Is Proclaimed by His Predestination

The term *predestination* is sometimes a controversial word. Sermons on that word have led to church splits and even cost some pastors their jobs. A friend once asked me to go out to lunch with him and talk about predestination, free will, and election. You know ... the little stuff. As we sat down and I started sharing some of my thoughts, he stopped me.

"Just so you know," he said, "I don't believe in predestination."

His is not an uncommon objection. I think that many people feel that way. The only problem is that predestination is a term found in the Bible, right here in Ephesians 1:5, "he *predestined* us." I mentioned that to my friend and told him that not believing in predestination is not an option for the believer who takes God's Word seriously. Where our disagreement may lie, I suggested, is in how we define the word.

Predestination broadly means "to decide beforehand." Our challenge is to understand what Paul meant when he used this word in Ephesians

1:5. Let me reconstruct what I think he is saying here. First, remember that predestination is one of the reasons God is to be blessed (v. 3). Therefore, predestination must refer to something *God did*, not to something he merely knew about or responded to, and not to something someone else did.

Second, God's predestination of us was done "before the foundation of the world" (v. 4). We must not miss the significance of this point. Why is Paul concerned that we know that God's choice of us was done before the foundation of the world? I believe it is so that we know that this act of predestination was not part of the natural world of cause and effect. It is hard to understand the significance of being removed from the world of cause and effect. When I do premarital counseling, I ask the betrothed couple to tell me the story of how they "got engaged." I have never had a couple come into my study and say they don't have a story. I have never heard, "We just met in the hallway and decided to come in here and ask you to marry us."

There is always a story. The boy loved the girl from afar for many months. The girl finally noticed the boy one day when he tripped in front of her. They began to talk, he won her over, his breath was bad and so were his jokes, but he was persistent. They broke up once, but he convinced her mom to sneak him in the back door during Thanksgiving dinner and she was so surprised to see him that she dropped the cranberry sauce and started to cry and he cried and—cause, effect, cause, effect, cause, effect and so on until I'm dedicating the latest effect on a Child Dedication Sunday. We live in a world of cause and effect.

Paul removes God from the world of cause and effect in describing his adoption of us. Before you existed, God predestined you. Nothing acted upon God to compel him to care for the spiritual orphan.

And therein lies a truth nearly impossible to get through our heads: *we, spiritual orphans, had nothing to do with our adoption.* Nothing! There is nothing we can point to within ourselves and say, "Here it is! Here is what God found worthy in me!" Instead, we look at God's choice of us and utter one word: grace!

I would explain predestination this way: God planned in eternity past what he would do with his creation, specifically, the plan that he has regarding salvation. His plan is to glorify himself. How did he plan to magnify himself in eternity past? By saving us.

Think about this: The heavens are a tremendous proclamation of the glory of God. In the early hours of November 19, 2002, I was driving to Chicago. Out of the corner of my eye, I saw what seemed to be a shooting star. As I turned, I saw another. And another. And another. Soon the sky was full with a magnificent Leonid meteor shower. I pulled the car over to the side of the road, turned off my lights, and sat in silent wonder at the vastness of our universe. But the greatness of the cosmos is not the primary way God planned in eternity past to display his glory.

On April 27, 2001, my oldest child was born. As I saw my daughter for the first time (after being assured by the doctor that the smurfish-blue color was a good thing), I was filled with wonder at the miracle of life. But the beauty of a newborn baby is not the primary way that God planned in eternity past to make his glory known.

The foremost way that his glory is manifested is by his glorious grace in saving you and me. This is the first reason God's grace is seen to be glorious: he predestined us for adoption.

God's Glorious Grace in Our Adoption Is Proclaimed by His Provision

Like my friends Robert and Grace, God did not just *plan* to care for orphans—he did it! He provided the resources that were necessary in order to care for them. The second reason God's grace is proclaimed in our adoption is because of how he provided for it. Ephesians 1:5 says that he predestined us *to adoption through Jesus Christ to himself*.

In the Roman culture, an adoption occurred when a nobleman who had no heir decided to become the benefactor of another man's son. He would purchase and then release the boy twice. After purchasing the boy for a third time, the nobleman would become the boy's father. This was a costly process for the nobleman, but through it he gained a son and the son, a father.

God's care for we who were spiritual orphans was costly as well. The provision that he made could not have cost him more—it was the provision of himself. When we say that Jesus Christ provided himself, we mean, first, he provided himself as the *means* to be reconciled to God and, second, that since he is God, he is also provided as the *goal* of reconciliation. First Peter 3:18 succinctly describes the provision for and goal of reconciliation: "For Christ also suffered once for sins, the righteous for the unrighteous, that he might bring us to God, being put to death in the flesh but made alive in the spirit."

The beautiful story of our adoption proclaims, first, that Jesus' death—the righteous dying in place of the unrighteous—provided the payment that our sin required. Second, it proclaims that his death "brought us to God." This truth is one that should bring us immense joy and security. "If you want to judge how well a person understands Christianity," argues J. I. Packer, "find out how much he makes of the thought of being God's child, and having God as his father. If this is not the thought that prompts and controls his worship and prayers and his whole outlook on life, it means that he does not understand Christianity very well at all."[1]

The care that God calls us to give to orphans will be costly at times. "Many of our children have special needs," one adoptive mother wrote to me, describing the difficult things God had called her family to do.

> We have had to learn to deal with learning disabilities, attention deficit issues, cleft lips and palates, and hearing impairments. The surgeries to correct the cleft lips and palates were hard to go through, but temporary. The syringe feedings and warm water soaks for repaired lips were especially painful. It was hard to see my baby trying to crawl with arm restraints on her little arms. It was difficult to take away her cloth that she loved to chew on to provide comfort. It was bitterly painful to watch her face bleed when the bandages were pulled off of her beautiful face. One daughter has had seventeen surgeries.... Another daughter still has a few surgeries to go.
>
> Yet another daughter came to us at almost ten years of age. Because she didn't have proper corrective hearing aids as a little child, she never developed a language. She is gifted at picking up on social cues, but she never learned to comprehend language. After a year of working with a Chinese tutor, hearing support, and English as a Second Language, we learned that she never acquired an initial language. After four years of tedious work, she can understand and speak much like a two-year-old. Is that difficult to deal with? Of course it is. But she is also a gift to our family.

How can families give of themselves like this? Because they rightly recognize the costly provision that God has made for them. As this woman observes, "Considering the impact on eternity that is being made, the difficulties of the adoption process pale very quickly."

The costs that are demanded of you as you care for the orphan may be high. Do not be surprised! Your Father paid a high price for you as well. We must not forget that or become complacent about that truth.

God's Glorious Grace in Our Adoption Is Proclaimed by His Pleasure

Do you believe God grimaced when you became his child? How do you picture him when you think of him bringing you into his family?

---

1. Packer, *Knowing God*, 201.

Ephesians 1:5 tells us that his adoption of us was "according to the purpose of his will." The word "purpose" can also be translated "good pleasure." God was not coerced into making us a part of his family. He receives us as his children not reluctantly but joyfully.

In the months preceding Ellie's adoption, we felt a great deal of anguish. The process of adopting from Guatemala was becoming more and more unstable; the government threatened to halt adoptions, including those that were already in process. The Internet became a mixed blessing. The rumor mill would begin flying. "Guatemamas" would frantically post on their blogs, and it was difficult to get a true sense of what was going on with the adoption process. It was quite a feat to essentially stalk government officials on a different continent.

Following those months of uncertainty, we brought Ellie home and there was rejoicing. The celebration took place not only in our own home but throughout our church and extended family. This precious one who had been an orphan was an orphan no more. She was with the family that would remain her family for the rest of her life. In bringing her home there was joy and laughter and excitement. So it is with God. He takes those of us who had been separated from him due to our sin and he welcomes us into his family with delight. And so is his glorious grace proclaimed.

The Glorious Grace of God Proclaimed by Our Response to Grace

God's grace will be a theme of our worship for eternity (see, e.g., Rev. 5:9). That grace of God will be seen as glorious as we contemplate how he predestined, provided for, and took pleasure in his care for we who were orphans. His grace will also be proclaimed by our response to it.

In Matthew 18, Jesus tells Peter the story of two slaves in order to demonstrate the riches of God's grace manifested by his forgiveness. One of the slaves owed a great debt to his master. The other owed a smaller debt to a fellow slave. Jesus tells Peter that the one who owed the great debt was forgiven, yet refused to forgive the other slave. As we care for orphans, we demonstrate the same grace that has been shown to us. A person who fails to manifest lavish grace proves he has not truly understood the magnificence of the grace given to him. In fact, a person who fails to live a life that manifests the grace of God calls into question whether or not he has received God's forgiveness. A person who has received God's grace through forgiveness has a sense of obligation to joyfully manifest that grace in the lives of others.

We Proclaim God's Grace by Recognizing His Grace

One of the most powerful ways that a person demonstrates compre-hension of Christ's work in his life is by radically altering the direction of his life. The believer is the one who receives God's grace, repents, and lives a life of grace as she rejoices in her forgiveness. The unbeliever fails to proclaim God's grace and even accuses God of malfeasance.

There are some people who are confronted with the brutality of humanity and conclude that God is either not truly good or not real. Elie Wiesel, a holocaust survivor, portrays the horror that was endured by the Jews in concentration camps in his novel *Night*. At one point, the narrator says, "Never shall I forget that night, the first night in camp, which has turned my life into one long night, seven times cursed and seven times sealed.... Never shall I forget those moments which murdered my God and my soul and turned my dreams to dust. Never shall I forget these things, even if I am condemned to live as long as God himself. Never."[2]

I cannot begin to fathom what it must have been like for Wiesel and the millions of others who endured the holocaust. What they went through was so horrific that for some it was as though God had been murdered. Yet others, who also endured the horrors of the holocaust, were able to see the glory of God in their suffering. In *Tramp for the Lord*, Corrie ten Boom recalls the moment when she came face to face with a former guard. "I have become a Christian," he told her. "I know that God has forgiven me for the cruel things I did there, but I would like to hear it from your lips as well. Fraulein ... will you forgive me?"[3] There was an intense struggle within her heart, but she was finally able respond:

> "I forgive you, brother!" I cried. "With all my heart." For a long moment we grasped each other's hands, the former guard and the former prisoner. I had never known God's love so intensely as I did then. But even so, I realized it was not my love. I had tried, and did not have the power. It was the power of the Holy Spirit as recorded in Romans 5:5, "...because the love of God is shed abroad in our hearts by the Holy Ghost which is given unto us."[4]

Corrie ten Boom's God was not killed in the holocaust but glorified in the darkest moment of modern times.

I pray that God grows my faith and understanding of his grace so that

---

2. Wiesel, *Night*, 34.
3. Ten Boom, *Tramp for the Lord*, 56.
4. Ibid., 57.

I would respond as Corrie ten Boom did. By faith I recognize that I cannot view the totality of the created realm and therefore I cannot declare God unjust in how he has dealt with humanity. In Scripture, Job looked at his experience and, after bearing the scrutiny of his friends, questioned God's decision to afflict him. Based upon his limited understanding, such testing seemed unfair. God responded to Job by challenging him to compare his own power, strength, and insight with God's. "Where were you when I laid the foundation of the earth?" asks God (Job 38:4). Only God has complete knowledge of the expanse of human history, and so only God rightly knows how individual events are part of his plan.

My point is that God is not painting on a canvas with a single paintbrush and one color. He is weaving a tapestry of grace with threads of various colors, shades, and hues. Here he uses the thread of pain; here the thread of suffering; here joy. The threads that the Lord uses in his tapestry are not always the ones we would choose. If we were able, we would perhaps offer suggestions regarding the colors to be used or protest his decisions. "Not the thread of despair!" we might cry. But such complaints would be at odds with the choices our Sovereign Lord has made. The tapestry is his tapestry. Someday, we will have the ability to step away from the thread of our lives and look upon the work as a whole. I firmly believe—even as I weep at the threads of pain and suffering woven into the lives of those around me—that the great theme of this tapestry will be the glory of God due to his grace. He will receive all the accolades and honors and praises that he is rightly due. We proclaim the glorious grace of God when we live in recognition of that incredible truth.

We Proclaim God's Grace by Providing for the Fatherless

We could touch upon many examples of how we proclaim God's grace, but we will focus simply on how to proclaim God's grace as we care for orphans. Caring for orphans is not just for the super-spiritual or those weird adoption advocates in the church. As we have already seen, orphan ministry is God's call on all believers. Engaging in this ministry, the "good work" of orphan care, proclaims God's grace to those around us. Jesus says that good works manifest God's glory to others; others see the good works and recognize their ultimate source. "In the same way, let your light shine before others, so that they may see your good works and give glory to your Father who is in heaven" (Matt. 5:16).

James's words in his epistle should be convicting for evangelicals who are only theoretically committed to ministries of mercy. James chastises those who would claim to be of the faith but fail to offer those things that should flow from a heart transformed by faith:

> What good is it, my brothers, if someone says he has faith but does not have works? Can that faith save him? If a brother or sister is poorly clothed and lacking in daily food, and one of you says to them, "Go in peace, be warmed and filled," without giving them the things needed for the body, what good is that? So also faith by itself, if it does not have works, is dead. (James 2:14–17)

An attitude of indifference does not proclaim God's grace. It fails to convince anyone of the reality of our professed faith. The one who merely offers words of encouragement to those in trouble—"Hang in there, buddy!"—without personally investing in meeting their needs does not have a faith that is vibrant and alive.

Still Not Interested

If you are a leader at a church and your church has no coordinated plan to provide for the orphan, you are failing to take advantage of a ministry God has called the church to do. I am not saying that your orphan ministry needs to or should look like our church's orphan ministry, but you need to obey God's Word in some way. The sad truth is, writes Timothy Keller, "Most of us have not come to grips with the clear directive of Scripture that *all* Christians must have their own ministry of mercy. We must each be actively engaged in it ourselves."[5]

If you have no desire to care for orphans, you have a profound spiritual problem. Let me be very frank, in a loving way. If you hear of the plight of the fatherless and tell them, in James's words, "be warmed and filled," without doing anything, there are some tough questions you need to ask yourself about your passion to see God's grace exalted.

SMALL GROUP DISCUSSION GUIDE

FELLOWSHIP AND PRAYER

STARTER QUESTIONS

1. How do compassion ministries help the church and individuals proclaim the gospel?

---

5. Keller, *Ministries of Mercy*, 43.

2. What are some ways you have seen God's grace displayed to unbelievers through an orphan care ministry?

SCRIPTURE TO CONSIDER

1. Review Ephesians 1:5–6.
2. Read 1 Peter 2, and focus especially on verse 12. How might this chapter change the way we view the purpose of difficulty and suffering in light of our overall purpose to point others to God's grace? What are the implications for orphan care ministry?
3. Read Matthew 18:23–34. Discuss ways in which the believer should demonstrate that he or she has received God's grace.

REVIEWING PRINCIPLES FROM THE CHAPTER

1. How did God provide for our adoption?
2. Review the three ways that God's glorious grace is proclaimed by his adoption of us. How is his grace proclaimed by his *predestination* of us? By his *provision* for our adoption? By his *pleasure* in our adoption?
3. How are we called to respond to God's grace? What are the characteristics of a person who has received God's grace?

APPLICATION QUESTIONS

1. How can you improve in your response to the grace you have received? Be specific.
2. How might you be called to provide for the orphan? Are you preparing for the physical-emotional-financial-spiritual cost of caring for the orphan?
3. Are there ways that you have already experienced the pleasure of caring for the fatherless?
4. How does emphasizing God's grace change our focus in orphan care ministry?
5. What can a church to do to ensure that its compassion ministries stay focused on God's grace?

4 A Theology *of* Adoption

When my grandfather was a teenager, he used to sneak from Mexico into Texas by swimming across the Rio Grande River," my friend told me. "He didn't tell his parents because he knew they would disapprove. He lived in constant fear that they would discover his secret.

"But one day, they did find out. And when he came home that evening, they sat him down and looked sternly at him. He shifted nervously around in his seat, wondering what his punishment would be. He was worried not only because of their wrath but because he knew this meant his job in the U.S. would be lost as well.

"'Son,' his father said with a cross expression on his face. 'You should not be sneaking across the border. It is dangerous and wrong. You should have talked to us before doing something so foolish.' His father paused. 'What is more, sneaking across the border like that is completely unnecessary.'

"'What do you mean?' he asked.

"'You have a U.S. birth certificate. You're an American citizen. You were born while we were travelling in the States, so you have all the rights of an American citizen. You don't have to sneak across the border! Walk through the border check like the American you are!'"

When my friend's grandfather found out this truth, it altered his life forever. Likewise, understanding who we are as God's adopted children is life-changing spiritual truth.

This chapter, "A Theology of Adoption," is first about *your* adoption— if you are a believer—and then about the implications of that reality for your care of orphans. Our relationship with God, restored through spiritual adoption, shapes our theology of earthly orphan care.

In particular, we will examine truths from the book of Romans that have dramatically shaped the vision and direction of our orphan care ministry.

Paradise—and Relationship—Lost

The restoration of our relationship with God through adoption provides us a theological lens through which to understand human adoptions.[1] By looking at God's adoption of us, we can learn how we are to respond to the needs of the orphan. Throughout Scripture, we are called to be imitators of God (e.g., 1 Cor. 11:1; Eph. 5:1; 1 Thess. 1:6) and our care of orphans should emulate the care our loving heavenly Father has shown us.

When Adam and Eve sinned, they lost not just paradise but also their relationship with God. The Bible tells the story of the restoration of paradise and, even more importantly, the story of the restoration of our relationship with God.

Salvation in Scripture refers to both deliverance from the future penalty of sin and deliverance from the immediate effects and power of sin. But the gospel is more than the good news that we have been saved from hell and the power of sin. It is the proclamation that our relationship with God has been restored and he is now our heavenly Father. We have been adopted. In this chapter, we will consider six truths regarding our adoption from the book of Romans.

Our Adoption Was Accomplished Despite Our Condition

I have a great dislike for germs. Being a parent of four young children who touch everything and put things in their mouth "just because" has presented someone like me with two options: go insane or learn to cope.

I tend to vacillate between the two.

When one of my children recently decided to multitask by brushing his teeth while going potty, he failed to grasp the importance of being careful. The toothbrush fell in and had to be fished out. Unfazed, he picked it up and continued brushing his teeth. After I found out about it, the poor kid was more likely to get sick from the Listerine antiseptic mouthwash he may have accidentally consumed than the infected toothbrush.

The truth I have come to begrudgingly accept is that the world is covered with germs. The University of Arizona found that your desk at work

---

1. There are an increasing number of works in the evangelical community that help us understand human adoptions by looking at the restoration of our relationship with God through spiritual adoption. For example, see Russell D. Moore, *Adopted for Life: The Priority of Adoption for Christian Families and Churches* or Dan Cruver's material at the Together for Adoption Web site, http://www.togetherforadoption.org.

is more germ-infested than the bathroom. In fact, on average there are 20,961 germs per square inch in an office—a desk alone can support up to 10 million kinds of bacteria. Other bacteria-laden substances in the workplace include the phone (25,127 germs per square inch), keyboards (3,295 germs per square inch), and computer mice (1,676 germs per square inch). How many germs are on the average toilet seat? Only 49 per square inch.[2]

For someone like me who has an innate phobia about all the disease-ridden people around me, the pervasiveness of germs is just a truth with which I have had to come to terms—and I have. Mostly.

Germs are a great illustration of sin. Like germs, sin is everywhere. No corner of our heart is sin free. Every inch of our being in some way violates God's commandments.

The first truth regarding our adoption by God is that our adoption was accomplished despite our condition (Rom. 3:10–23). The picture painted of humanity in Scripture is often very bleak, and few passages convey the depth of our sin more thoroughly than Romans 3:10–23. "As it is written: 'None is righteous, no, not one; no one understands; no one seeks for God. All have turned aside; together they have become worthless; no one does good, not even one,'" Paul begins. Throughout the rest of the passage, he draws truths from various Old Testament sources, primarily the Psalms, to convey our depravity.

This idea that sin pervades our being is sometimes called "total depravity." It does not mean that we are doing every evil thing we could possibly do at all times, but rather that there is no part of us that is left unaffected by the fall. Paul is not simply exaggerating for effect. He is quite clear: None is righteous . . . no one seeks for God . . . no one does good. Each of us has a real problem with sin.

In college, I worked for a man whom I admired because of his love for the Lord. Once, I remarked to my boss that one of the amazing things about God's grace was that we cannot fathom the depth of God's forgiveness. He disagreed, and with tears in his eyes told me that he knew that he was a terrible sinner. The depth of his sin, he claimed, was continually before him.

I graciously agreed with him that he was a terrible sinner. But I also held my ground. He was a far greater sinner than he knew. I believe he was sincere in his sorrow for his sin but naïve concerning its depth. The reason I believe that is because of what we have just read in Romans 3. We do not understand the ways in which we constantly transgress the righteous instructions of the Lord. In fact, one of the remarkable things about our

---

2. Williams, "Is Your Desk Making You Sick?"

growth in grace is that we continue to grow in our understanding of what terrible sinners we are. Don Whitney asks the probing question:

> Are you aware of sins in your life that you weren't cognizant of years ago, even though you were committing those sins back then as well? As discouraging as the fresh exposure is, and as grievous as it may be to have ever-deeper layers of sin laid bare, there's something positive here. Increased sensitivity to your sin is a mark of growth.[3]

What we first learn from Romans was that our adoption by God was done while we were immersed in sin. As we grow in grace, this is a truth of which we become more painfully aware.

> *The implication for earthly orphan care is that there are no unlovable children.*

In the novel *Anne of Green Gables*, nosy Mrs. Rachel Lynde finds out that her neighbors, Matthew Cuthbert and his sister, Marilla, are planning to adopt a child. She is thoroughly opposed to the idea. She scolds Marilla, and as she does so she expresses thoughts that many have had but have been afraid to express out loud:

> Well, Marilla, I'll just tell you plain that I think you're doing a mighty foolish thing—a risky thing, that's what. You don't know what you're getting. You're bringing a strange child into your house and home and you don't know a single thing about him nor what his disposition is like nor what sort of parents he had nor how he's likely to turn out. Why, it was only last week I read in the paper how a man and his wife up west of the Island took a boy out of an orphan asylum and he set fire to the house at night—set it on purpose, Marilla—and nearly burnt them to a crisp in their beds. And I know another case where an adopted boy used to suck the eggs—they couldn't break him of it. If you had asked my advice in the matter—which you didn't do, Marilla—I'd have said for mercy's sake not to think of such a thing, that's what.

When people begin to consider caring for orphans, it is inevitable that they will run into the Mrs. Lyndes of the world. And it is hard to argue

---

3. Whitney, *Ten Questions*, 103.

with the basic premise that caring for orphans is a risky thing. You often do not know anything about the child you are bringing into your home nor what the child's future holds. Fear of the unknown causes many to decide they would rather not care for orphans at all than risk getting a "rotten egg"—or a child who sucks on eggs.

May God forgive us for such arrogant thoughts! Those who think along these lines, like the man I worked with, have not come to grips with the depth of their own rottenness.

I would like to offer you my personal guarantee: if you decide to care for the orphan in any way, even to the point of adopting her and bringing her into your home, that child is going to have "issues." Sometimes those issues may be so profound that God will use them to break your heart at its very core.

Brett and Hillary are an ordinary couple who have been involved in extraordinary things. Shortly after adopting their second child, Hillary says, "God placed children with HIV on my heart." I think it is fair to say that most of us would be at least initially reluctant to seek to adopt a child who was HIV-positive. Hillary had similar misgivings:

> I questioned God and tried to convince him that he had the wrong gal. Yet throughout the next year HIV seemed to be everywhere I turned—news, articles, books, and stories on this disease were brought to my attention. Slowly, I was becoming educated on HIV and my heart began to become more and more burdened for those living with this disease.
>
> On November 21, 2007, the local news channel broadcast a video hoping to locate a family for a sixteen-month-old little boy in need of a forever family who would be willing to love him just the way he was and willing to advocate for him for life. This little boy was HIV-positive and I knew he was to be my son.
>
> On March 24, 2008, HIV moved into our home. Along with it came a miracle—our son. We finally held "more of Jesus" . . .

To me, one of the most powerful things about Hillary's testimony is her frank assessment of why she was reluctant to care for a child with such special needs. "It's embarrassing to admit this," she writes,

> but part of the reason why I was so afraid to say yes to our son was because I had this fear that he might not be *perfect*. You know, all parents want their children to be perfect. I know it's silly, but

we do. We want everyone else to gush over our children, to say how cute they are, how they act like little angels, well mannered, polite, and respectful. We want them to be straight-A students, popular, well-rounded, athletic, strong.

It's every parent's dream.

And, well, while viewing our son's files and the challenging circumstances he was coming from, I'm ashamed to admit that I was afraid. Someone told us that we were "taking on someone else's problem" and I was afraid that they might be right. But you know what? I was wrong. *Dead wrong.*

God does not make mistakes and God made our son. He brought him to final form, and our son has suffered because of someone else's sin. He is ... total, made in the image of God....

And I almost missed this because of my warped American view of perfection.

Are you in danger of missing out because of your warped view of perfection?

If God could look upon us—depraved enemies of God—and offer us salvation, how dare we put some children in the category of "unlovables"? Are we willing to look at a boy or a girl and say, "Because of your gender or color or deformity or age or ability or past, I will not love you"? I say it again: May God forgive us for such delusional arrogance!

That does not mean that love is easy, or that every believer is called to adopt troubled or disabled children. Far from it! What it does mean is that we should not put up barriers within our hearts and refuse to be receptive to the needs of those whom God places in our path. Furthermore, it means that as we make decisions regarding who and how to help, we must be careful to examine our motives for making the choices we do.

Repent of the idea that there was something about you that was so beautiful that God said, "Wow! I must have him for my collection!" God's adoption of you was not *because* of your condition but despite it.

Our Adoption Was an Act of God

Romans 3:24–26 further explains that our adoption was an act of God:

[All] are justified by his grace as a gift, through the redemption that is in Christ Jesus, whom God put forward as a propitiation by his blood, to be received by faith. This was to show God's righteousness, because in his divine forbearance he had passed over former sins. It was to show his righteousness at the present time, so that he might be just and the justifier of the one who has faith in Jesus.

Our justification—or being declared righteous by God—came about by God's grace. It was a gift. This gift could only be brought about by the work of Christ and can only be received through faith in him. God, therefore, is the "justifier of the one who has faith in Jesus." God declares us righteous as he deals with our sin in a way that only he could.

> *The implication for earthly orphan care is that we must be proactive with our love.*

Children are not provided for by their own initiative but by the intervention of others. Ellie had no choice in whether or not she would become a part of our family. She did not get a referral of us to consider. She did not have a chance to interview our family, or to decide if the cold Midwest was where she would like to end up. We were the ones who made that decision for her. We filled out the paperwork. We accepted the referral. We decided to love her. We decided to bring her into our family. Our love for her was initiatory. We love God because he first loved us, and if we had not first loved Ellie, she would never have loved us.

Our Adoption Was Accomplished Through the Suffering of Our Savior

The third truth from Romans we will reflect on is that our adoption was accomplished through the suffering of our Savior. The suffering of Christ was not accidental. It was part of the premeditated and predetermined plan of a loving God to bring about our salvation. Paul describes this plan in Romans 5:6–11:

> For while we were still weak, at the right time Christ died for the ungodly. For one will scarcely die for a righteous person—though perhaps for a good person one would dare even to die— but God shows his love for us in that while we were still sinners, Christ died for us. Since, therefore, we have now been justified by his blood, much more shall we be saved by him from the wrath of God. For if while we were enemies we were reconciled to God by the death of his Son, much more, now that we are reconciled,

shall we be saved by his life. More than that, we also rejoice in God through our Lord Jesus Christ, through whom we have now received reconciliation.

It was "at the right time" that "Christ died for the ungodly" (cf. Acts 2:23; Eph. 3:1–11). The suffering of Christ came about at the exact moment God had planned for it to come about in order to purchase us for himself.

We have a perception that suffering is a bad thing and should be avoided at all costs.[4] When making a decision, often one of the criteria we use—subconsciously or consciously—is the amount of discomfort such a decision will bring to us personally. If it will inconvenience me, it is "bad," if it will make my life easier, it is "good."

Scripture forces us to alter our evaluative system. While we are not called to seek out suffering, we are told that it is "through many tribulations we must enter the kingdom of heaven" (Acts 14:22) and "all who desire to live godly in Christ Jesus will be persecuted" (2 Tim. 3:12).

> *The implication for earthly orphan care is that caring for orphans is going to cost you.*

Do not deceive yourself into thinking that caring for orphans will always be a blissful, enjoyable ministry full of emotional satisfaction. There will be moments that are trying. Caring for orphans will cost you your time. It will cost you financially. It will cost you your ease of life. If you already have children, it may cost them as well. This is the price of obedience, and it is a price we pay gladly as we consider the treasure we are pursuing (2 Cor. 4:17).

Count the cost now. Understand that God calls his people to do tough things. His adoption of you was not something done on the cheap. It cost him the life of his only Son. Our earthly care of orphans will be costly as well.

Our Adoption Makes Us a Part of a New Family

My wife comes from a family of three girls. Whitney is the oldest, followed by Amanda, then Grace.

When they were little girls, Whitney and Amanda thought it was great fun to tease Grace. One of the things they used to tell her was

---

4. For the way in which this understanding of suffering affects orphan care, see chapter 7, "The Greatness of Godly Affliction."

that she really belonged to another family at their church, the "Smith" family. They were one of those families who were very sweet but a little ... unusual. Their clothes were out-of-date. Their social skills were awkward, and they were unaware of it. The children had interesting quirks and personalities that tended to make for some uncomfortable situations. The parents were boring but it didn't stop them from monopolizing a conversation.

Grace knew what her sisters were doing. They were implying that she was a little "unusual." By saying that she was not one of them, they were attacking her conception of herself.

Being part of a family is significant. It provides a sense of identity. When you describe your family, you are describing something about yourself. As people find out about your upbringing they can understand you more. Being part of a family also provides a sense of security. We can lose our health, our freedom, our money, but one of the enduring things in life is family. No matter how much you like or dislike the members of your family, they cannot (truthfully) claim that you are not theirs!

The fourth truth to examine in this chapter is that our adoption makes us a part of a new family. The believer finds identity and security in his new relationship to God:

> For all who are led by the Spirit of God are sons of God. For you did not receive the spirit of slavery to fall back into fear, but you have received the Spirit of adoption as sons, by whom we cry, "Abba! Father!" The Spirit himself bears witness with our spirit that we are children of God, and if children, then heirs—heirs of God and fellow heirs with Christ, provided we suffer with him in order that we may also be glorified with him. (Rom. 8:14–17)

Notice several things here that the Holy Spirit does in regard to our adoption. First, his presence assures us that we are part of God's family. Those who have become part of his family have the Spirit, who serves as a comforter and aide, residing within. Second, he allows us to be brought closer to God. We can cry out, "Abba! Father!" only because of the testifying work of the Spirit. Third, the presence of the Holy Spirit confirms our status as sons of God. In the Roman culture, it was the son who was the heir of his father. To be called sons of God means that we have the assurance that comes from being his heirs. The Spirit is a down payment on that future inheritance (Eph. 1:13–14). The great truth of Romans 8 is that by a divine act we have been made a part of God's family.

There may be times when we struggle with this truth. We have been transferred from a kingdom of darkness to God's family, but we may still sometimes feel as though we are part of our old family. For the true child of God, it is helpful to remember that our emotional acceptance of that fact does not affect its truth. Though we may not always feel it to be true, the objective reality is that all who place their faith in Jesus Christ are children of God. We used to be children of wrath; we are now children of God (Eph. 2:1–3)

> *The implication for earthly orphan care is that orphaned children may struggle with their family identity.*

I'm sure you think you have a great family, but I have to admit that I think mine is better. There is no other family in the world of which I would rather be a part. My children sometimes disagree and mention to me that another family looks like a lot of fun. "Boy, at Andrew's house they eat cake all the time, play outside, and never have to go to bed. I wish we could be a part of Andrew's family!" As you may imagine, these moments of desiring to be in another family are more likely to occur when they are eating vegetables instead of cake, doing chores instead of playing outside, and going to bed instead of staying up late.

When they express dissatisfaction with the hardships associated with being my child, I lovingly tell them, "Tough!" It does not matter what their desire at that moment is because I am their father. And I trust that they find great comfort in the reassurance that they have an identity and security in our family.

A child who was an orphan may also struggle with the fear that she is not truly part of the adoptive family. Even when she has parents who love and care for her, that does not mean she will readily accept that family as her own. Indeed, she may struggle with identity and security her entire life and be forced to rely more fully upon God to help her through times of doubt.

I was once talking with a man about our plans to adopt. During the course of our conversation, he shared with me that he had been adopted. He believed his father loved him and had cared for him, and they had a good relationship. But he still did not believe that the love his father had for him was the same as the love he had for his biological children. As I told him that we planned to adopt, he said these words: "You will never love your adopted child the way you do your biological children. You will say you do, but you won't."

Even years removed from his childhood, this man still struggled with a sense that his place within the family was different from the place occupied by the biological children. I am not sure how accurate his perceptions were, but even in the best circumstances, it is not unreasonable for an adopted child to struggle with doubts.

The truths found here in Roman 8 encourage us as we care for orphans. Orphans may struggle with their place within a human family, but God's adoption of us gives us confidence because as his children we are in a permanent family structure.

Our Adoption Can Never Be Revoked

There is something that is true about Ellie that is not true for any of our other children; I can never disinherit her. Before finalizing her adoption, one of the requirements was that we had to sign a document stating we would never write her out of our will. Even if I wanted to disinherit her—which I would not—I could not. Financially, it would not be a great travesty for any of our children to be written out of our will. But I like the feeling of permanence it provides for Ellie. Our adoption by God is even more binding.

The fifth encouraging truth from Romans is that our adoption can never be revoked:

> And we know that for those who love God all things work together for good, for those who are called according to his purpose. For those whom he foreknew he also predestined to be conformed to the image of his Son, in order that he might be the firstborn among many brothers. And those whom he predestined he also called, and those whom he called he also justified, and those whom he justified he also glorified. ... For I am sure that neither death nor life, nor angels nor rulers, nor things present nor things to come, nor powers, nor height nor depth, nor anything else in all creation, will be able to separate us from the love of God in Christ Jesus our Lord. (Rom. 8:28–30, 38–39)

In these two passages in Romans 8, note the permanency of our union with God. In verses 28–30, he oversees every step of the process as we are brought into an eternal relationship with him. It is he who foreknows, who plans, who calls, who justifies, and who glorifies. Our security rests not on our own efforts but on God's sovereign oversight. In verses 38–39, based upon his confidence in the work of God at every step, Paul draws this conclusion: There is nothing that can separate us from God.

The implication for earthly orphan care is that our love for the fatherless must be enduring.

I would like to offer an encouragement to those who may be struggling with loving an orphan or an adopted child. God does not necessarily call you to respond with certain emotions. He calls you to respond with love. Sometimes, as we care for orphans—especially when we have adopted children—there can be fear on our part as we notice our emotions are different.

Our culture, sadly, is awash in unbiblical understandings of what love is. In romantic relationships, we confuse lust with love. Or we believe we love someone because of how that person is able to meet our emotional or physical needs. Or we believe the fairy tales that teach us love is some mysterious force that exists outside of ourselves and sweeps us off our feet. These are fleeting loves. Lovers who base their confidence in their relationship on such an unbiblical understanding soon find themselves uttering unbiblical phrases like "falling out of love" as if love were some sort of tree in which one perched precipitously.

The essence of true, biblical love is choosing to sacrificially care for another person. In orphan care, love means committing to care for a child no matter what. God's love is demonstrated for us in the fact that he brought us into his family despite our condition. Understanding that biblical love is not an emotion but a conscious choice can help us through the struggle of caring for children.

Parents have sometimes confessed to me that they are unsure as to whether or not they love their children. Those who have adopted are unnerved as they feel certain emotions that they do not think should be there, or lack certain emotions that they think they should have. I encourage these parents to pursue bonding activities with their children, but at the same time I offer them a more biblical understanding of what love is. I ask them if they have committed to sacrifice of themselves for the benefit of the child. If they have, they have committed to the foundational characteristic of biblical love in that relationship.

The truth to be gleaned in this portion of Romans 8 is to continue to persevere in your love for the orphan. Even when times are tough—even when it feels as though a breaking point has been reached—carry on.

Paul's words in Galatians 6:9 should stir within you a godly desire to persevere: "And let us not grow weary of doing good, for in due season we will reap, if we do not give up." Now is not the time to quit. Do not grow weary of doing good. The love that God has for us and the love that he enjoins us to have toward the orphan forbids us from ceasing in our efforts to care for them. Will you continue serving at an orphanage when the children despise you? Will you continue to sponsor a child when you hear discouraging things about what is taking place in her life? Will you love the foster child who steals from you? By God's grace, yes.

Our Adoption Is for the Glory of God

The understanding that the purpose of life is to glorify God permeates this book. Therefore, it should come as no surprise that we close with this thought and explore once again another implication of this truth. There are numerous passages in Romans that illustrate this, such as Romans 15:7. As Paul discusses how the believers in Rome should conduct themselves, he harkens back to the theme of their entrance into the family of God and applies it to hospitality: "Therefore welcome one another as Christ has welcomed you, for the glory of God." (Rom. 15:7).

Hospitality in Paul's culture was more involved than having someone over for lunch after church. It was an involved affair in which one lavishly provided for the aid and comfort of the guest. The guest's feet were washed, several meals were provided, lodging was given. The model for hospitality is Christ. He has welcomed us into his family, lavishly providing for us, and we are to emulate him for the glory of God.

> *The implication for earthly orphan ministry is that we are motivated to care for orphans for God's glory, not our own.*

We must be careful to search our motives as we pursue caring for children. We must not be motivated by pride, loneliness, guilt, or anything other than the glory of God. The orphan is embraced not so that we can receive credit but so that the name of God can be exalted.

When my friend's grandfather found out that he had been born in the United States, it was a source of great joy for him. No longer was he a foreigner, he was a citizen. Opportunities opened up for him that changed his life. Similarly, knowledge of how we became a part of God's family should change our life as we think about how it will affect our care for the fatherless.

Small Group Discussion Guide

Fellowship and Prayer

Starter Questions
1. As we conclude part 1, what are some of the truths that have had the biggest impact on your understanding of how and why God cares for orphans?
2. Do you have a greater sense of the ministry God may be calling you to as you think about caring for the orphan?
3. What questions or topics do you want to make sure are covered in the coming weeks of the study?

Scripture to Consider
As you review the principles from the chapter in questions 2–7 below, read the related passages from Romans that correspond to each section.

Reviewing Principles from the Chapter & Application Questions
1. Why does studying truths regarding God's adoption of us help us in considering how to care for orphans?
2. What does it mean that our adoption was accomplished "despite our condition" (Rom. 3:10–23)? What was our condition? What are the implications for our care of orphans?
3. What does it mean that our adoption was an act of God (Rom. 3:24–26)? What did he do? What are you willing to do to care for the orphan? What are some things that God may ask you to do that you are not prepared for? What are some other implications of this truth on our care for the fatherless?
4. What does it mean that our adoption was accomplished through the suffering of our Savior (Rom. 5:6–11)? What are some ways that you or your family may suffer as a result of trying to care for the orphan? How can you begin to prepare yourself for that? Have you talked with people who have been through difficult circumstances in orphan ministry? How have they been able to persevere in their ministry?
5. What does it mean that our adoption makes us a part of a new family (Rom. 8:14–17)? How can you use God's Word to encourage a child who struggles with accepting their adopted family?
6. What does it mean that our adoption can never be revoked (Rom. 8:28–30, 38–39)? How does that encourage you in your spiritual

life? How can that truth encourage the orphan? How can that truth be used to encourage adoptive parents (i.e., what issues do adoptive parents struggle with that this truth can address)?

7. How does the truth that our adoption was for the glory of God affect an orphan care ministry (Rom. 15:7)?

PART TWO

God's People
and the
Orphan

In part 1, we learned important principles concerning God and his love for the orphan. In this second part, we will consider God's call on his people to care for the orphan.

God's people—the church—have been adopted by God. As adopted children, they are now part of a new family that is knit together by Christ. This second part will look at how those who are part of this divine family should respond by caring for the orphan and why the spiritual family of God is uniquely equipped to care for the fatherless.

We will also see that we have a profound need to examine our own hearts as we contemplate whether or not we are spiritually prepared to care for orphans and if we are ready to joyfully endure the difficulty of this ministry. We will also examine how we can make God-honoring decisions as we pursue caring for orphans.

The final chapter of part 2 will explore how we should approach church leaders when we desire to begin an orphan care ministry. This chapter will help committed lay people encourage their leaders to joyfully pursue God's call to care for the fatherless.

5 Blessings, Missions, *and* Orphans

As I was leaving a reception for a young couple preparing to depart for the mission field, I poked my head into the sanctuary to tell them goodbye and found a scene in which deep sorrow was mixed with inexpressible joy. Only the family of the couple was left in the room. Eyes were filled with tears as brothers and sisters and moms and dads said goodbye. The couple was going to a dangerous area, and no one knew when they might see each other again. I waited outside for an appropriate moment to say goodbye.

The scene affected me deeply. Why would the couple sacrifice a relatively comfortable life and take up a life of difficulty? What would possess them to cause such pain? The answer, of course, is that there was something greater to be gained. There was something more valuable than an easy life or pleasing one's family. The gospel is so precious it calls us to sacrifice everything for the cause of Christ.

Every church I have ever been a part of has understood the value of missions. They rightly understand that missions—the proclamation of the good news of Jesus Christ—is an essential component of what God has called them to do.

In this chapter, we explore just three of the many reasons that missions and orphan care ministry are similar. I am not arguing that a church that involves itself in an orphan care ministry has fulfilled its missions commitment. Rather, my contention is that a church that engages in orphan care ministry is engaging in an essential component of missions work.

Missions and Orphan Ministry Both Rely Upon God's Blessings

The first reason that missions and orphan care ministry are similar is that both are dependent upon God's material blessings. We see this truth dramatically proclaimed in Psalm 67.

Materialism Kills Missions

Missions and orphan care ministries both rely upon God's people understanding why he blesses the church materially. Sadly, many wolves in sheep's clothing have infiltrated the church and taken advantage of the flock. For the love of money, they engage in ministry for their own gain.

In 2005, *The Fifth Estate*, an investigative news journalism program, aired an exposé on Benny Hinn, a member of the Word of Faith healing movement.[1] One segment of the program focused on the story of an eight-year-old girl named Grace. Grace was born with a variation of muscular dystrophy and is confined to a wheelchair. The documentary chronicles her attempts to attend a crusade and be healed. Sadly, little Grace and her mother were not allowed anywhere near the stage.

There is a movement within Christianity that has been given many names. Some call it the "prosperity gospel" or "health and wealth gospel" because it promises physical health and material prosperity. Others call it the "Positive Confessions movement" or "Word of Faith movement" because of its teaching that we can somehow command the sovereign God of the universe by speaking words of faith. One popular pastor calls a slightly less insidious version of it "Your Best Life Now."

All of them share one thing in common: They have perverted the gospel of Jesus Christ as it was once for all delivered to the saints. And though many believers are deceived by it, the peddlers of this perversion stand guilty of selling, literally, a false gospel—one where they have displaced Christ from the center of the gospel and have exalted the temporary above the eternal. They have made the means to an end the end itself.

I feel a profound sense of sadness for what Grace has gone through. I ache as I think about the emotional pain and disappointment she felt that night. But I am more concerned—I am crushed—as I think about the spiritual damage that might have been done to her.

Imagine, instead, if Grace had been told about the real Jesus Christ that night. What if she had been told that there is someone who can satisfy her more than being able to walk? What if she had been told that Jesus Christ is more valuable than any physical or material gift that she could ever hope to receive?

What false gospel are you peddling by the way you understand the relationship between physical resources and the gospel? The

---

1. As of the time of the publication of this book, the documentary, "Do You Believe in Miracles?" could still be found at http://www.cbc.ca/fifth/miracles/index.html

health-and-wealth peddlers are wrong because they are hocking a false gospel for material gain, but we who are in love with our homes and cars and clothes and electronics and other trinkets are guilty of abuse of material possessions as well because we fail to understand *why God has given us material things.*

A right understanding of missions and orphans ministry demands that those of us who have been materially blessed understand why God has blessed us. We must not trade Christ for a trinket. We must not sell the all-surpassing worth of the Savior for a worthless souvenir.

American materialism is a damnable gospel, and for those of us who have bought into it, let me offer a variation of Peter's very strong words to Simon in Acts 8: If God does not turn your heart, may your gold and silver perish with you because you thought the ultimate gift of God was money instead of himself.

Why God Has Blessed You Materially

Psalm 67 offers a radically different message. If the North American church embraced this message, it would radically change her ability to do missions and care for orphans. The message of the psalm is this: God blesses you *so that* his gospel will be proclaimed to all peoples *so that* they will joyfully worship him. God blesses you *so that* he will be glorified through missions. The gospel is proclaimed by God's people as they use his physical blessings to increase the joy of all people through worship.

The Structure of Psalm 67

¹ May God be gracious to us and bless us
    and make his face to shine upon us,   *Selah*
² that your way may be known on earth,
    your saving power among all nations.
³ Let the peoples praise you, O God;
    let all the peoples praise you!
⁴ Let the nations be glad and sing for joy,
    for you judge the peoples with equity
    and guide the nations upon earth.   *Selah*
⁵ Let the peoples praise you, O God;
    let all the peoples praise you!
⁶ The earth has yielded its increase;
    God, our God, shall bless us.
⁷ God shall bless us;
    let all the ends of the earth fear him!

The psalms are poetic works, originally written in the Hebrew language. Unlike popular poetry today, Hebrew poetry in the Old Testament is more concerned with ideas than with sound and rhythm. The Hebrew poets often employed parallelism, where one section of the poem is compared or contrasted with another section, such as when a second line expresses ideas similar to the first line. In verse 2, for example, the phrase "your way may be known on earth" is parallel with the phrase "your saving power among all nations."

Another characteristic of some Hebrew poetry is called chiasm. Chiasm is rather like throwing a boomerang—you end where you started, covering the same ground in reverse order on the way back. In a chiastic structure, the main idea is at the center of the poem—the point where the boomerang reverses—instead of at the beginning or end.

This is what happens in Psalm 67. Observe the following layout:

A. God, bless us so that you may be known on the whole earth (vv. 1–2)
>   B. Let the peoples praise you (v. 3)
>>   C. Let the nations be glad and sing for joy (v. 4).
>   B^1. Let the peoples praise you (v. 5)
A^1. God blesses us so that he is known on the whole earth (vv. 6–7)

Observe the "boomerang." The psalm begins and ends by talking about God's blessing. At the center we find the main theme: the joyous worship of God by the nations.

The bookends teach us about God's grace. The bookends of the psalm, labeled A and A^1, show us several things. First, the Lord is the one who graciously gives all things. The psalmist rightly recognizes that God is a sovereign giver. His appeal in these verses is to God, asking him to grant his blessing. The psalmist does not arrogantly presume that what he has is due to his own ingenuity or labor; he acknowledges that it is from the Lord.

Furthermore, the Lord is not a miserly giver. The psalmist uses words and phrases—"gracious," "bless," "may your face shine upon us," and "the earth has yielded its increase"—that show the bounty of God's gifts, The psalmist does not ask for some table scraps and leftovers. He asks God to graciously bestow abundant *physical* gifts upon his people.

The bookends also teach us about the purpose of gifts. Gifts are given so that God's message can be communicated. The blessings of God allow his way to be known over all the earth. And, of course, "all peoples" includes orphans. In other words, orphan ministry uses material means to reach spiritual ends.

The middle sections teach us about the purpose of missions.
Missions is not an end in itself. It is a means to an end.[2] Verses 3 and 5 show
us that the result of using our material possessions to proclaim the greatness of God should be that the recipients too acknowledge the greatness of
God in worship—"Let the peoples praise you!"

The center teaches us about the end result of missions. The central section of the psalm in verse 4 shows the people worshipping God not
out of obligation but out of joy. The missions task, of which orphan care is
a part, could be summed up this way: *In missions and orphan care ministry, we
use our worthless, temporary material possessions to help proclaim the immeasur-
able value of Christ, so that others can engage in joyful worship of him.*

Think of the relationship between material blessings, missions, and
worship as similar to the relationship between a proposal, an engagement,
and a marriage. I began dating Whitney in high school. We dated through
college and then, after graduating, I proposed to Whitney on January 10,
1999. The entire day was focused on honoring my future bride. The dinner,
the walk in a park, and the poem I wrote her were all very enjoyable, but
not my ultimate goal. In fact, the ultimate goal of my proposal was not even
merely to get a "yes" from her. The "yes" only got us to the next stage of the
relationship: the engagement.

The engagement was an important part of our relationship. But it too
was not the ultimate goal. Everything was a means to the goal of marriage.
A proposal allows us to enter into an engagement, which leads to marriage.
Material blessings allow us to engage in missions, which leads to worship.

You Are Wealthy

Some may protest, "Well, I am glad you are telling rich people to use
their money for missions. They need to use their resources for the gospel.
But me ... I'm barely making ends meet! Leave the serious giving to the
wealthy!"

If those are your thoughts, I have some good news for you: You are the
wealthy! According to the Global Rich List, if you make $20,000 a year,
you are in the top 12 percent of wealthiest people in the world.[3] If you
earn $30,000, you are in the top 7.5 percent. A mere $60,000 puts you
in the top 1 percent. Anything above $125,000 a year puts you in the top

---

2. Piper, *Let the Nations Be Glad*, 17.
3. To find your own position on the Global Rich List, visit http://www.global-
richlist.com.

0.5 percent of wealthiest people in the world. You get the idea. Let me be the first to congratulate you on your newfound wealth!

Sadly, the more people earn, the less of their income they give. Studies show they become more immersed in the things of the world.[4] It is imperative that you ask yourself this question: Why has God made me so wealthy? What do his blessings mean? Did God make me wealthy so that I could accumulate more material possessions than others? Or, perhaps, did God grant me material possessions so that I could demonstrate his worth to those around me by gladly parting with those treasures in order to pursue him?

For your own benefit and joy, give generously. It is rare that even the poor in our North American culture cannot afford to give at least 10 percent of their income. As your income increases, what sacrificial giving looks like changes in terms of what percentage of your income you are able to give. If people making $70,000 a year give 10 percent of their income, they are still wealthier than 99 percent of the people on the planet. People making $200,000 who give 10 percent of their income still have access to more resources than 99.85 percent of the people on the globe.

Find the standard of living to which God has called you. Then, as the amount of money you make increases, do not increase your standard of living. Instead, increase your standard of giving. Randy Alcorn exhorts believers to have a "strategic" lifestyle. This means that they can still enjoy the resources that God has provided, but they do so with an understanding of why God has provided those resources. As your income increases, consider this mind-set: "I won't look at my income as God's call to spend more, but rather as his provision to invest more in the cause. I might determine to live on a certain amount of money each year, an amount that allows some room for discretionary or recreational spending. All income beyond that I will give to God's kingdom purpose."[5]

This is the practice Alcorn has adopted, which means "if [God] provides twice the amount of money I've designated for my living expenses, then I'll give away 50 percent of my income. If he provides four times that much, I'll give away 75 percent."[6]

God blesses you so that his gospel will be proclaimed to all peoples so that they will joyfully worship him. I pray that God gives you the grace to give and experience the joy that comes from participating in his kingdom plans through your stewardship. May orphans who today do not know the

---

4. See Brooks, *Who Really Cares.*
5. Alcorn, *Money, Possessions and Eternity*, 301.
6. Ibid.

Lord be able to engage in worship of God next to you in heaven as a result
of your faithfulness in sacrificial giving.

Missions and Orphan Ministry Both Proclaim the Gospel

The second reason that missions and orphan care ministry are related
is that both must proclaim the gospel of Jesus Christ (1 Cor. 15). I once
had a conversation with a man who was struggling with some doctrinal
disagreements he was having with some other believers. His concern was
that he not sacrifice the unity of the church over debatable matters. As we
talked, we decided to first consider what the core doctrines of the faith
were. We both agreed that the gospel, the good news of Jesus Christ, is the
most important truth that has been entrusted to the church.

There are numerous differences of opinion that can occur between
brothers and sisters in Christ on various issues, but there can be no difference of opinion concerning the essential tenets of the message of salvation.
It is imperative that the church hold firmly to its proclamation that salvation is through faith alone in Christ alone.

Therefore, it is crucial that the message of reconciliation be proclaimed by all facets of an orphan care ministry. Evangelical churches that
care for orphans must be careful to invest their resources in ministries that
meet the spiritual as well as the physical needs of orphans. By all means,
spend great amounts of effort to meet tangible, physical needs, but in your
zeal to meet those physical needs, do not become distracted from your
ultimate goal. Missions and orphan care ministries must clearly proclaim
the gospel of Jesus Christ.

Our goal is not to share "the minimum amount of truth to the maximum number of people" but "the maximum amount of truth to the maximum number of people."[7] If the gospel is dislodged from the center of
your ministry, you have failed in your goal to proclaim the good news of
Jesus Christ to all people.

The gospel cannot be jettisoned or compromised. The last half of the
previous century saw evangelicals compromising the integrity of the gospel in order to maintain peace with fringe elements of Christianity. This
was true especially with movements within evangelicalism that depended
upon a variety of churches and denominations coming together in order to
be successful. The price was steep. There was a failure to clearly proclaim

---

7. Metzger, *Tell the Truth*, 33.

the good news of Jesus Christ, and divisions occurred regardless. As Iain Murray observed:

> The best remedy then for divisions among Christians is for all to put first the living and teaching of the gospel. An all-around failure to do this by evangelicals in the last fifty years has undoubtedly played a part in divisions which have occurred.... David Wells is surely right when he says: "The most urgent need in the church today, even that part of it which is evangelical, is the recovery of the Gospel as the Bible reveals it to us." When Christ is put first, when making disciples of all nations is the first priority, division is far more likely to occur where it should occur, between believers and the world.[8]

Do not for the sake of pragmatism join with groups that do not share your commitment to the gospel in caring for orphans. There are a lot of items we can debate, or at least avoid discussing for the sake of unity, but the gospel is not one of them. It is a uniquely important message and the cornerstone of our ministry. For this very reason, Paul delivered the gospel as the message of "first importance" (1 Cor. 15:1–22).

At this point I would be remiss if I did not ask you to carefully consider the state of your own soul. Who are you trusting for your salvation? As you contemplate the day of your departure from this earth, upon what do you base your hope of salvation? Scripture is clear that you must trust in nothing else but Jesus Christ. God was pleased to punish Christ in your place so that now you may accept the free gift of heaven by faith alone in Christ alone.

Do not build your adoption ministry on something besides the gospel message. This is the message that must be proclaimed to orphans as they are cared for inside or outside your home.

Missions and Orphan Ministry Both Result in Ethnically Diverse Worship

Once upon a time, my daughter Hannah told me the story of two bugs who lived in a field across the street from our church. Their names were Hannah and Austin (coincidentally, the same names of our two oldest children). One day, Hannah Bug and Austin Bug decided to go to church. They hopped across the parking lot and had to watch out for cars. They

---

8. Murray, *Evangelicalism Divided*, 310.

had to have someone open the door for them because they were too small to open it for themselves. As they walked through the halls, they were so tiny they were in constant danger of being trampled. When they got to the sanctuary, they had to sit in an area where no one would accidentally sit on them and squish them.

Unfortunately, my daughter continued, at one point in the service, an old lady noticed the two bugs and began to scream. Pandemonium ensued as the whole church began to yell and shout and people ran around the sanctuary. Hannah Bug and Austin Bug were in mortal peril. But the pastor noticed the two bugs and scooped them up and put them onto the pulpit so they would be safe and could hear the message.

What a great picture of church from the viewpoint of a little child. Church is a big place, and the church must take steps to proactively care for our younger members, ensuring that little people feel welcome and are not "stepped on."

Similarly, the church must take proactive steps in order for there to be ethnic diversity in the church's worship. Diversity will not occur by happenstance. We must want it to happen. We must reach out to those of other ethnicities to make them feel welcomed within our walls.

Missions and orphan care ministries should both result in ethnically diverse worship of God. A day is coming when prejudice, racism, ethnocentrism, and all other race-related sins are coming to an end, and the church will experience perfect unity as we submit ourselves completely to our head Jesus Christ.

In Psalm 87, God demonstrates a desire for diversity in worship.[9] His goal of ethnically diverse worship fuels our passion for missions. We want to see a diverse group of people worship God. As we engage in caring for orphans, we begin to see God's vision for ethnic unity realized. In Psalm 87, we see three principles regarding diversity that influence our understanding of missions and orphan care.

God Delights in Ethnically Diverse Worship

First, God delights in ethnically diverse worship. We read this in the first three verses of Psalm 87: "On the holy mount stands the city he founded; the LORD loves the gates of Zion more than all the dwelling places of Jacob. Glorious things of you are spoken, O city of God." God desires to bring together people from various cultures to worship him, and in these verses, the psalmist conveys this by telling us that God has a special love for

---

9. My understanding of Psalm 87 was heavily influenced by Ron Allen's article "Psalm 87: A Song Rarely Sung."

Zion's gates. The gates were the points of entrance for worship, and God is excited that worshippers from various people groups are entering through them.

Some might argue that diversity is a by-product of proclaiming the gospel and not necessarily a goal in and of itself. However, the delight of God in this psalm reveals that diversity *itself* is a goal.[10] God doesn't want just a bunch of white people or brown people or black people or mauve people worshipping him.

The delight God has for diversity in worship is seen in both the Old and New Testaments. For example, in the Old Testament, in Solomon's prayer of dedication for the temple, he asks God to listen to the prayer of the foreigner "in order that all the peoples of the earth may know your name, to fear you" (1 Kings 8:43). The psalmist envisions a time when "peoples gather together, and kingdoms, to worship the Lord" (Ps. 102:22).

In the New Testament, the Great Commission is not a command to just reach a large numerical population but to reach all the nations, or "ethnos," meaning people groups. In Revelation we see the fulfillment of this command as people from all ethnicities are worshipping God. "After this I looked, and behold, a great multitude that no one could number, from every nation, from all tribes and peoples and languages, standing before the throne and before the Lamb, clothed in white robes, with palm branches in their hands" (Rev. 7:9). It is "all nations" who "will come and worship" God and exalt his "righteous acts" (Rev. 15:4). These passages envision the gospel message being delivered not just to individuals but to ethnic groups as well. All people groups are called to enter into corporate, unified worship of God.

God's People Are United Through Rebirth

The second principle from Psalm 87 is that God's people are united through rebirth. In verses 4–6, we see something rather astonishing. Unity consumes diversity as one is reborn in Zion. Watch who comes through the gates: "Among those who know me I mention Rahab and Babylon; behold, Philistia and Tyre, with Cush—'This one was born there,' they say. And of Zion it shall be said, 'This one and that one were born in her'; for the Most High himself will establish her. The Lord records as he registers the peoples, 'This one was born there.'"

Despite being from a variety of places, our common citizenship due to our rebirth binds us together in a way nothing else could. The psalmist

---

10. See Piper, "The Supremacy of God Among 'All the Nations," *Let the Nations Be Glad*, 155–200.

mentions five groups of people who know God: Rahab (or Egypt), Babylon, Philistia, Tyre, and Cush (or Ethiopia)—and they are all united in worship of Yahweh. In fact, they are considered "Zion born."

Royal cities would have a register listing the citizens of that city, and membership had its privileges. Citizens were exempt from some taxes, exempt from military duty, and benefited from magnificent building projects. Here is a listing of people of whom God declares, "This one was born there"! These enemies who were born in other parts of the world have been "reborn" and are now considered citizens of Zion.

God Saves His People Through Exclusive Means

True diversity will not take place through man-made ends. Instead, true unity takes place through diverse groups coming to place their faith in the Christ. In Psalm 87:7, we see that even though a variety of people come to worship Yahweh, the springs of salvation are found in Jerusalem alone. "Singers and dancers alike say, 'All my springs are in you.'"

The third principle is that God's plan of salvation is exclusive. In the psalm, an Egyptian cannot find salvation in Egypt. A Babylonian cannot find salvation in Babylon. The truth claims of the God of the Jews are unique. All are invited in and can worship God as equals—provided they come through the gates of Zion.

Believers sometimes express a reluctance to engage in certain types of ministry to the fatherless. At the root of their resistance is a heart that is committing the sin of ethnocentrism. The goal of diversity in worship is achieved in profound ways through orphan ministry. As we partner with people from different ethnic backgrounds to care for orphans, we are experiencing the unity Christ calls us to have. As we bring children into our homes from different ethnic backgrounds, our earthly family begins to resemble the eternal family of which we are a part. This must be the desire of a transformed heart that loves to hear God worshipped.

SMALL GROUP DISCUSSION GUIDE

FELLOWSHIP AND PRAYER

STARTER QUESTIONS

1. How has God blessed your church/community/country materially?
2. Why do we sometimes not feel very wealthy?

Scripture to Consider

1. Read through Psalm 67. What might it say if it were written to our culture? What are some ways we might ask God to bless us materially?
2. Read through 1 Corinthians 15:1–11 and discuss the central tenets of the gospel.
3. Review Psalm 87.

Reviewing Principles from the Chapter

1. Why has God blessed us financially? How does our poor stewardship of our physical resources undermine the gospel?
2. What essential truths should be communicated when sharing the gospel?
3. Why does God delight in ethnically diverse worship? Do you share God's delight for this type of worship? Why do you believe the church so often fails to experience this aspect of worship if God delights in it?

Application Questions

1. Do you believe you are using God's resources the way he desires you to? What are some areas in which you believe you are doing well? In what areas are you perhaps being a poor steward? Do you have a budget that you are following that reflects God's priorities?
2. Do you understand how to clearly communicate the gospel message to a non-Christian? What would you say?
3. How can we ensure that the gospel message remains at the core of our orphan care ministry? What are some ways we might be tempted to compromise the gospel message?
4. What are some things you can do to increase the ethnic diversity of the worship in your church?
5. Is it possible that racism is limiting the types of orphan care ministry of which you are willing to be a part?

6 When Not to Care *for* Orphans

One evening, my father refused to allow my brother and me to participate in family devotions. We had exchanged harsh words (and perhaps more) with one another and so as we came into the living room on this particular night to pray together and read the Bible with the rest of the family, our hearts were far from an attitude of worship. As he examined the scowls etched on our faces, my dad realized we were not prepared to approach the throne of grace. He told us to leave the room while the rest of the family prayed together. Though sometimes I would have loved to get out of family devotions, this was not the manner in which I had envisioned my escape.

I was stunned and—to my surprise—began to protest loudly that Dad had no right to ask me to leave. He had no right, I declared, to refuse to let me participate in devotions. I needed to pray and read the Bible! Dad remained resolute and told me I could not worship with the family until I had resolved the situation with my brother. We were so distraught that our previous differences were forgotten, the situation was quickly resolved, and we were allowed to return. My shock, however, had been genuine and profound, and impressed upon me the truth that one cannot approach God cavalierly. One's heart must be prepared to revere him as the sovereign king that he is.

There are moments in Israel's history when her people are told not to go through the motions of worshipping God because of the condition of their hearts. Through the prophet Malachi, God declares that he wishes sacrifices would not be offered in his temple: "Oh that there were one among you who would shut the doors, that you might not kindle fire on my altar in vain! I have no pleasure in you, says the LORD of hosts, and I will not accept an offering from your hand" (Mal. 1:10). Israel's worship is so half-hearted that God wishes someone would bar the doors to prevent this charade from taking place. His call on the people is to first prepare their hearts, then engage again in worship. Fortunately, Malachi tells us, some responded to the Lord's rebuke and became his "treasured possession."

Some of you should not care for the orphan. Like the people of Israel, you will need to examine your heart to see if there are areas that God needs to refine before you engage in caring for the fatherless. What you read in the following pages may be difficult and may cause you pain, but it may also prove to be the most helpful chapter for you in the long run.

Do Not Care for Orphans if You Are Practicing Idolatry

Your friend and her husband sit on the couch across from you in your living room. She looks down at her hands, which are in her lap holding a tissue. Her husband looks at her with a pained expression on his face. Occasionally, his hand will reach over and pat hers. It is obvious they are hurting. They desperately want children and have just suffered another miscarriage. Despite several procedures over the past several years, they have encountered failure again. Their struggle now, they tell you through tears, is whether or not to continue with some rather difficult and expensive medical procedures—or pursue adoption.

Your friend shares that she has had significant struggles over the past year and a half. She has been battling depression, loneliness, jealousy, and even anger. In her opinion, all of these troubles stem from her inability to have children. As she finishes discussing her medical options, she sighs and tells you, "You know, I will do whatever I have to in order to have children. I know I will not be happy until I hold my own baby in my arms. Maybe that is God calling us to adopt."

Your heart aches for this couple. Perhaps you have even personally experienced their pain and know many others who have as well, but as they discuss the different options that are available to them at this point—such as adoption—you feel a sense of unease. Is it possible that this couple, who has already been through so much, is not spiritually prepared to care for the orphan? Is it possible that children have become an idol for your friend?

What Is Idolatry?

The essence of idolatry in Scripture is to place our highest affections upon something other than God. Sometimes this is done consciously and deliberately as we call something "God" that is not God, as we craft for ourselves a god that is like the god we desire. There are numerous examples of this in Scripture. For example, Moses warns the people against fashioning a God for themselves:

> Therefore watch yourselves very carefully. Since you saw no form
> on the day that the LORD spoke to you at Horeb out of the midst

of the fire, beware lest you act corruptly by making a carved image for yourselves, in the form of any figure.... Take care, lest you forget the covenant of the LORD your God, which he made with you, and make a carved image, the form of anything that the LORD your God has forbidden you. For the LORD your God is a consuming fire, a jealous God. (Deut. 4:15–16, 23–24)

Idolatry is not just the fashioning of an object to worship, however. Even good desires like peace and security and children can become idolatrous as they become the focus of our hearts. The fruit of this idolatrous affection manifests itself as our actions betray what is in our hearts. James gives us a foolproof test to see whether or not we are practicing idolatry:

What causes quarrels and what causes fights among you? Is it not this, that your passions are at war within you? You desire and do not have, so you murder. You covet and cannot obtain, so you fight and quarrel. You do not have, because you do not ask. You ask and do not receive, because you ask wrongly, to spend it on your passions. You adulterous people! Do you not know that friendship with the world is enmity with God? Therefore whoever wishes to be a friend of the world makes himself an enemy of God. (James 4:1–4)

When we want something and do not get it, our behavior will reveal our idolatry. If I love money so much that I become angry when my portfolio suffers a loss, my response shows that I am worshipping money instead of God. When I have a sinful response because of what my heart desires, it reveals that I love something more than I love God.[1]

Consider just a few illustrations of this principle. It is not wrong to want peace in your home. But how much do you desire peace? If you want it so badly that you will respond sinfully if you do not obtain it, it has become an idol. As you rant or rave or scream or seethe, know that such a response reveals you are worshipping peace. You want it more than God. Your desire has become idolatrous.

Or consider the desire to have your spouse love you. Such a desire in and of itself is certainly not a sinful desire. In fact, it is something that God commands your spouse to do, therefore your desire here conforms to God's

---

1. My application of this passage is greatly influenced by Brent Aucoin's series entitled, "The Heart of Change." DVDs of his series can be obtained through the Faith Biblical Counseling Ministry at http://www.frlafayette.org.

desire for your spouse. How will you respond, however, if he or she does not act in a loving manner toward you? Your response reveals whether or not the desire has become idolatrous. It shows whether or not your desire for your spouse's love is greater than your desire to honor God.

Our responses of despair, fear, anger, frustration, and the like are constant warning signs that show us that whatever is evoking this response has become an idol. Our problem is compounded by the fact that the human mind is, as John Calvin put it, "a perpetual forge of idols."[2] The task is to be an idol smasher, constantly analyzing the conflicts and upsets in your life and trying to discern what your heart is worshipping at that moment.

I have some very wise friends who have taken this truth to heart. They are idol hunters in the best sense of the term. They have adopted four children and are constantly on the hunt for idols in their own lives. The husband, Jim, told me that he is amazed to find out the things his heart loves more than the Lord. "I thought I was just frustrated because our kids were misbehaving. Then I realized it was because I was worshipping my own comfort. As I analyzed the moments of frustration, I realized it wasn't just my comfort I was worshipping. I was also worshipping my pride. I took it as a personal affront that my child would defy me." It is an ongoing battle in his heart—and the hearts of all believers who wish to worship God—to detect idols, confess them as sin, and respond in faith.

How Does Idolatry Relate to Orphan Care?

Idolatry is an obstacle that must be confronted when considering caring for orphans. It can be difficult to distinguish between God-honoring motivations and idolatrous motivations. This means that we must be willing to lovingly ask ourselves and those whom we love difficult questions as we assess our spiritual readiness to engage in ministry. Let me give just a few hypothetical scenarios that illustrate this concept, and then we will look at the biblical solution.

Chad. Chad recently lost his job of seventeen years as his company struggled to face "challenging economic realities." A talented engineer, Chad had struggled for several years as he felt a sense of discontentment in his work. He often complained that he did not receive the recognition he deserved. His boss and coworkers were frequently blamed for his failure to be promoted. It was not unusual for him to speak of conflicts at work. As Chad speaks about his former place of employment when asking others to pray

---

2. Calvin, *Institutes*, I, 11.8.

for him, he expresses a great deal of bitterness toward the company and the people who "abused" him so terribly.

A month or two after losing his job, on an Orphan Sunday, Chad was moved by a presentation at his church. He was especially interested in discussions related to overseas orphan care. The following month, Chad announced to his Sunday school class that he was going to pursue working at an orphanage overseas. He approached the church leaders with a request for support.

The leaders were torn. They were excited that someone would want to care for orphans, but also a little perplexed. Chad had never been involved in any ministry in the church before, nor shown any interest in ministry. To further complicate matters, he was sharing his plans in other Sunday school classes and asking for support from individuals.

How should the church leaders respond? Based on James 4, they should recognize that the conflicts Chad experienced indicate the real possibility that he is practicing idolatry. Perhaps he has an idolatrous desire for recognition and significance. The church leaders should ask him very direct questions about his calling. They should also ask him to prove himself faithful in ministry before laying hands on him for full-time missions work. His response will indicate much about his humility or his idolatrous desires.

Tim and Sarah. Sarah and her husband Tim have been married for seven years, and things are not going well. Both were previously married. Tim had been married for five years when his wife deserted him. Sarah had been married for seven years when her husband died of cancer. Each has two children from their previous marriages, and so their children range in age from nine to fourteen.

Their marriage is engulfed in conflict. Finances, parenting strategies, and dealing with Tim's ex-wife are constant battlefronts. Sarah believes that the problem in their marriage is that there is nothing that unites them. She suggests that taking in a foster child would be a good project for their family to participate in together to bring them closer to one another. Tim is so desperate for the conflicts to end that he is willing to try anything.

The presence of conflict again points us to James 4. What are the "passions" that are waging war within Tim and Sarah? Many more questions will need to be asked, but perhaps Sarah has an idolatrous passion for her family to look "traditional." Tim may love peace so much that he is willing to say or do anything to restore tranquility. Their unwillingness to pursue what is best for the other means they do not understand sacrificial love and are not prepared to engage in orphan care ministry at this point in time.

Brandon and Jill. Brandon and Jill have been married for twelve years. The first five years of marriage, they each focused on pursuing a career and paying off their school loans. After they paid off those debts, they began to try to have children. For the first two years of trying, Jill was not discouraged. But as the years continued without a pregnancy, she became more and more desperate. She and Brandon consulted various specialists, and with each failed procedure it seemed less and less likely that they would ever have children. There are months into which Jill sinks into a deep depression, unable to shake feelings of gloom and despair. Eventually, she decides that the only way she will be able to have children is through adoption.

When you talk with Jill, she shares with you that she is sad that they cannot have biological children. "Adoption is not my first choice," she confesses. "But biological children are not an option. So many of my problems stem from not having children. If God would just give me children, I could be happy. In fact, I guess adoption is our last chance at happiness."

Jill's comments reveal an idolatrous desire for children. It is entirely possible that God may call her and Brandon to care for orphans, but their motivation must not be idolatrous. Those who love Brandon and Jill should encourage them to pursue God as their first love. Be willing to ask Jill if God would still be a loving and good God if she never had children. Furthermore, the perception that caring for orphans is a second choice needs to be confronted as well.

Debbie. Debbie is a passionate advocate for the orphan. Really passionate. In fact, many have used the term "over zealous" to describe her—and not unfairly. She frequently comes into conflict with those in leadership in the church who take a different approach to orphan care. She accuses them of lacking faith and not being obedient to God's commandments.

Remember James's words. What is the source of quarrels and conflicts? We want something that we do not have. Debbie's desire to see her church care for the orphan has become an idolatrous desire. The idolatrous nature of her desire is revealed in her confrontational, ungodly attitude.

How Idolatry Can Be Cured

I do not mean to imply that a person who is guilty of idolatry in the area of orphan care should never care for an orphan. I do not mean that those who care for orphans are idol free! Those who care for orphans must, however, follow the prescription given by God in James. His call on believers is to humble themselves and repent of idolatry:

Or do you suppose it is to no purpose that the Scripture says,

"He yearns jealously over the spirit that he has made to dwell in us"? But he gives more grace. Therefore it says, "God opposes the proud, but gives grace to the humble." Submit yourselves therefore to God. Resist the devil, and he will flee from you. Draw near to God, and he will draw near to you. Cleanse your hands, you sinners, and purify your hearts, you double-minded. Be wretched and mourn and weep. Let your laughter be turned to mourning and your joy to gloom. Humble yourselves before the Lord, and he will exalt you. (James 4:5–10)

God desires that we turn from the idols we have fashioned for ourselves and let the Holy Spirit rule within our hearts. As our hearts are humbled, we become consumed with a passion for God. We are able to look at the circumstances in our life as part of his plan instead of tenaciously clinging to our own design for our lives. As we grow in humility, our desire becomes to worship God, and we are then better prepared to care for the fatherless.

Do Not Care for Orphans if You Have Not Properly Counted the Cost

Many who think they are ready to undertake orphan care are completely unprepared for what awaits them. I'm about to use all caps, but even still, some of you will miss what I'm about to say because you don't want to hear it:

CARING FOR ORPHANS IS VERY, VERY, VERY, VERY HARD. IT IS ONE OF THE MOST HEART-WRENCHING AND EMOTIONALLY DRAINING ENDEAVORS YOU WILL UNDERTAKE.

In a fairy tale, despite whatever misery takes place after "once upon a time," the story always ends "happily ever after." Often those who have a desire to care for orphans view this ministry through fairy-tale-covered lenses. They watch adoption videos or hear a sweet song on the radio or read blogs and become enthralled with the possibilities of bringing a child home. I had lunch with a friend recently who commented on the difference between real-life adoptions and blog adoptions. The white-washed version of reality that we see of the ministry often fails to present the difficult side of orphan care.

Orphan care ministry is not a fairy tale. It is a God-glorifying tragedy. No matter how wonderful it is to care for a child who is an orphan, we cannot escape the tragedy that began the story. God will be glorified through the story and we will experience joy, but we must not allow the joy of caring for the fatherless to blind us to the difficulty of the ministry in which we are endeavoring to participate.

When I talk with people who seem to have an unrealistic concept of caring for children, I ask someone who has been involved in adoption and foster care to contact them. One woman I asked to share her testimony with a group hesitated. "I'm not sure you want me to do that," she cautioned. "I may convince them not to go through with it."

"That would be better than the alternative," I countered.

It is critical that people have the right understanding of what an orphan care ministry is and why God would call them to it. If someone who has been challenged as he has gone through the process of caring for orphans can warn others of the difficulties they may face, all the better.

A Difficult Question

The one who follows Christ does not trod an easy path. Joyful? Yes. Easy? No! In fact, Jesus encourages those who are considering following him to count the cost before doing so:

> Now great crowds accompanied him, and he turned and said to them, "If anyone comes to me and does not hate his own father and mother and wife and children and brothers and sisters, yes, and even his own life, he cannot be my disciple. Whoever does not bear his own cross and come after me cannot be my disciple.... So therefore, any one of you who does not renounce all that he has cannot be my disciple." (Luke 14:25–27, 33)

Before visions of cute children with frills and lace coming into your home fill your head, think realistically about what God calls you to as you follow him in discipleship. The man or woman who follows after Jesus in discipleship will first need to make a careful calculation and arrive at this conclusion: nothing compares with the infinite value of possessing Christ. I am confident that the person who counts the cost wisely will arrive at that conclusion, but until we do so, we are not prepared to follow after him in orphan ministry or any other ministry. So do not begin to care for the orphan until you have asked yourself, "Do I really want to be a disciple of Jesus Christ?"

The Desire to Be a Disciple: Luke 14:25–26a

Luke tells us that "great crowds" accompanied Jesus. It did not take a lot of effort to be a part of the crowd. In this story, Jesus is addressing those who desired to be his disciples. Jesus was a popular teacher, one who taught with authority, and offered healing to some. In the Gospels excitement for Jesus is at its height before people understand what he is really all about.

People came to Jesus, they surrounded him, and perhaps they assumed that they were his disciples. A disciple was one who not only listened to the teachings of the one whom he was following, but imitated the teacher's lifestyle as well. The disciple's goal was to live like his teacher.

Here Jesus lays out the terms of discipleship. He will not accept casual hangers-on who come and go as they please. He considers what is best for their souls and, with some very difficult words, exhorts the people to continue on.

The Cost of Being a Disciple: Luke 14:26b–33

Jesus could have just told those who were following him, "Look, to follow after me, you must love me very, very much. You must value me above all other things." But he didn't. Instead, he tried to help them understand the heart attitude of the one who would be a true Christ-follower. These words have significant implication for us as we strive to follow after Christ in the area of orphan care.

Hate your family. Step 1 in counting the cost of being a disciple of Jesus is to hate your family. If someone "does not hate his own father and mother and wife and children and brothers and sisters," he is disqualified from being a disciple. Jesus is using hyperbole—an exaggerated statement—to convey a radical truth. Jesus is in effect saying: If you desire to follow me, your love for me must be so great, so consuming, that you are willing to turn your back on even your family if they prevent you from following me.

What will your family say if you decide to go on a missions trip to an orphanage in a dangerous location? What will they say if you decide to take in a foster child in your golden years? What will your parents say about an adopted child who might inconvenience their current, biological grandchildren? It doesn't matter. Jesus says, just follow me.

If you desire to follow after Christ by caring for orphans, understand that it may mean you must "hate" your family in the sense that their value pales in comparison to Christ's. This may mean that you are willing to suffer the scorn of your parents who do not understand why you would sacrifice what seems like so much for what seems like so little. It may mean that

God calls you to do things that will greatly inconvenience your biological children and you must be willing to watch them suffer as you follow Christ.

In the summer of 2007, we took a missions trip to the orphanage in Guatemala where Ellie was living. We had planned the trip before we received our referral and were thrilled at how God worked out the opportunity to meet her before our adoption was finalized. But the trip seemed to be over as soon as it began, and leaving Ellie in the orphanage was one of the hardest things I have ever had to do. We put Ellie into the arms of one of the workers, got onto the bus, and I put my head in my hands and began to sob.

A few days after we got home, Whitney compiled a video montage of our trip and showed it to our other children. They laughed and giggled at all the right parts and were excited to see their little sister in action.

Then came the scene where we had to leave Ellie at the orphanage. Whitney looked over at our son Austin, who was four years old at the time, and was surprised to see tears, streaming down his little face.

"Why are you crying?" she asked.

"It's just so sad," he said. "I don't like it when you leave Ellie."

We would watch that video many times as a family, and Austin would cry every time. It broke his little heart to see Ellie left in Guatemala.

If we had decided not to adopt, we would have avoided inconveniencing our other children. If we had decided not to visit Ellie, we would not have felt the pain of leaving her. If we had decided not to show the video to the kids, we would not have caused Austin emotional distress. Our other children could have remained blissfully ignorant of the hardships that other children in the world face. But, oh, what a far greater loss our family would have experienced!

We cannot protect our children or loved ones from the pain of this world. They will share in our suffering. We must prepare ourselves for that reality and keep as our goal the surpassing joy of exalting Christ. Only in hating our family—considering their value as nothing compared with Christ's—can we truly love them.

Hate your life. Jesus adds that his disciples must hate even their own lives. If you desire to follow after Christ and care for children, it may cost you the life that you love so much. It may bring troubles upon you. It may cost you financially. You may not get to retire in Arizona. You may not get to take that trip to Paris you have been dreaming of. The little sports car of the future may need to be exchanged for the minivan of today.

At some point, Jesus will tell you that your plan for your life is not his plan for your life and you will have to answer the question, Do I love Jesus so much that I am willing to hate my plan and embrace him?

Why does Christ demand so much? Why must you hate your family and your own life? There is no other way to experience ultimate joy in Christ apart from properly valuing him. The one who values him properly inevitably hates everything in comparison with him. A person who has not arrived at the realization of Jesus' infinite value is not prepared to be his true disciple.

The value of orphan care ministry is not ultimately determined by the value of the children being ministered to. After all … we must "hate" the orphan as well! Instead, it is calculated by the worth of Christ and that value is demonstrated by the degree to which we are following Christ. His worth surpasses the value of our family, of our comfortable life, of our job, of the orphan—of everything!

The final words Jesus offers are strong: "So therefore, any one of you who does not renounce all that he has cannot be my disciple" (v. 33). Let that sink in for a moment. Are you ready to renounce all that you have in order to follow Jesus—especially in the area of caring for orphans?

Whatever you cling to most tightly shows what you most value. Jesus' value is infinite, and he wants us to understand that. He calls on us to consider his worth and rightly assess it and then live out that understanding. May God grant us the grace to refuse to value anything more highly than him and then to live out that devotion accordingly. Our parents, our spouse, our children—as wonderful as they are—are nothing compared with him. Our life's goals, ambitions, and plans must all be centered on him.

Following Jesus is costly but we do so joyously. Because Christ is superior to all other objects upon which we could bestow our affections, there can be no greater joy to be experienced in life than obtaining him. As we choose following Christ as we care for the orphan, we are beginning a difficult road of discipleship that will provide us with satisfaction we cannot even fathom.

Do not pursue orphan care ministry if you have not counted the cost. Orphan care ministry is tough. It is one of the toughest things in life you can do. If you do not value Christ highly enough, the price it demands may overwhelm you.

Do Not Care for Orphans if You Are Doing So on Your Own Strength

In 2008 I had the privilege of being involved in planting a new church. The task was enormous. We were not the typical church plant. Several hundred people from one church were involved in this endeavor, which presented us with both advantages and disadvantages. Because of our size, there was a need for a large number of workers for ministry. We estimated that in the area of children's ministry alone we were going to need about one hundred people engaged to some degree. Yet, because we were so new, we did not have all the necessary people trained and ready to go.

Relying Upon Our Own Strength

There are a variety of ways I could have motivated people to be engaged in the ministry God was putting before us. I could have tried guilt. I could have stressed how hard other people were working and how we needed each person to do their part. I could have told them that little children were never going to hear about Jesus unless they volunteered to be workers in the children's Sunday school class. I could have just begged until they felt sorry for me. Guilt and pity can be very effective tools in motivating others to do what you want.

The problem is that those who are in church leadership are responsible not just for the ministries we recruit people to but how we recruit people. Can you imagine our anguish if someday we find that our labors were in vain because we did not have the right heart attitude as we labored? What if our care for orphans proved to be useless because our motivation and heart attitude in our labor was wrong?

The truth I wish to convey is that *God calls and equips people to do work in his strength.* Philippians 2:13 reads: "for it is God who works in you, both to will and to work for his good pleasure." *God* works in *us.* As we do ministry, we continually rely upon him to enable us. Ministry cannot be done on our own. Part of his work is to give us the will—the desire—to do ministry. He creates within the heart of the believer a "calling" to ministry and simultaneously gives the believer the ability to carry out their ministry. Therefore, God takes pleasure in our ministry.

It is foolish to engage in orphan care ministry on our own strength. God directs his ministers as he will, and our responsibility is to follow his leading. Trying to force ourselves to do a ministry that God has not called us to will only result in frustration and failure.

Failing to Understand Spiritual Gifts

Imagine you opened a restaurant and dedicated yourself to finding the best chefs in the world. You invest millions of dollars in hiring these chefs and bring them to your restaurant. Too late, you realize that you should have hired some additional staff—like waiters and a maître d' and an accountant (who could have told you not to hire so many chefs). No matter how wonderful your chefs are, your restaurant will fail without some other staff.

God in his wisdom has given the church more than just chefs. He has placed in his body members who are equipped with a variety of gifts. In

1 Peter 4:10–11 we see some of the reasons why each of us should do ministry in God's strength and not our own: "As each has received a gift, use it to serve one another, as good stewards of God's varied grace: whoever speaks, as one who speaks oracles of God; whoever serves, as one who serves by the strength that God supplies—in order that in everything God may be glorified through Jesus Christ. To him belong glory and dominion forever and ever. Amen." Each believer has been given a gift and is commanded to use it to meet the needs of others. Believers are not masters of these gifts but stewards.

I am a frugal guy, and being forced to utilize valet parking is particularly irksome to me. But when forced to do so, even though I give my keys to a valet, there is a clear understanding that the car is still mine. He is to employ the use of that car under my directions. He does not have the freedom to do whatever he wishes with it. Similarly, we do not have the freedom to employ our gifts however we desire. We employ them under the direction of the one who gave them.

A church can apply this truth to orphan care ministry in several ways. It may be that people have a desire to help in the ministry in a way that is not being driven by the work of the Holy Spirit. Perhaps an individual is working in an area of orphan care ministry that God has not gifted her to be employed in. Or perhaps a pastor has a preconceived notion for how his church should care for orphans, but God has not provided the necessary people to carry out the vision for the ministry.

There are many indications that we are ministering in our own strength. Having a sense of entitlement can indicate self-fueled ministry. Hanging on too tightly to a ministry can indicate that the work is ours and not the Lord's. Feeling a sense of obligation instead of joy or being weary of the work are both indications that God's equipping strength is not being supplied in that ministry.

We must also remember that *our purpose is to glorify God with our gift.* Peter begins to conclude by stating that we do ministry in God's strength "in order that in everything God may be glorified through Jesus Christ" (v. 11). Peter's point is that if this is a ministry for which you are supplying the strength, it is to your own glory when things are accomplished. If, however, it is God who is equipping for ministry, then it is he who receives the glory for the ministry and its fruit.

Do Not Care for Orphans if You Are Discontent

Let me close by touching briefly on a topic that is closely related to what we looked at in the beginning of the chapter when discussing idolatry.

Sometimes people who desire to be involved in orphan care ministry are discontent.

When Whitney and I were relocating to the community where the church was going to be planted, we had a four-month gap between the time we sold our old house and when we moved into our new one. We longed to be in our new home and kept telling ourselves that things would be better once we got settled into the new house.

But as we waited to move, we became convicted that this was not the right way to think about our circumstances. Our problems would not magically disappear once we moved the last box into our new home. New problems were surely waiting for us just around the corner. The right response was to realize that contentment can be found in any circumstances as long as what we are seeking is the Lord. If you are not happy where you are right now because of your external circumstances, you will not be happy even when your circumstances change.

There are a number of reasons why people pursuing orphan care ministry might be discontent. They are adopting and want the wait for their child to be over. They are waiting to leave for the mission field and want their support to come in. They want the church to begin an orphan care ministry and are tired of the delays. Whatever the reason, they are unhappy with their current circumstances and believe that they will be happy when what they want finally comes to fruition.

The truth of the matter is that our external circumstances will never bring us joy. If we cannot learn to be content during difficult times, we will not be able to find contentment in times of ease either. Contentment is not found by getting the things that we want but rather in wanting Christ and pursuing him.

Paul tells the Philippians, "I have learned in whatever situation I am to be content. I know how to be brought low, and I know how to abound. In any and every circumstance, I have learned the secret of facing plenty and hunger, abundance and need. I can do all things through him who strengthens me" (Phil 4:11–13). Christ enables Paul to feel contentment even while in chains.

If you are considering adoption and believe that you cannot be content until you have that child in your arms, let me ask you a hard question: What are you going to do if God never allows that to come to pass? I pray that you come to the point where you can say, "As long as I have Christ, I can be content!"?

The Road Ahead

It is true that God has called his people to care for orphans. That does not mean, however, that going through the motions of obedience fulfills his call on our lives. There are numerous circumstances in which we should examine our preparedness to engage in orphan care ministry. If orphan care ministry has become an idol, we must first humble ourselves and worship God. If we have not counted the cost of providing for the fatherless, we must do so before brazenly engaging in ministry. If we are trying to do the ministry on our own strength, we must instead rely upon the strength God supplies through the gifting of his Spirit. Finally, if we are discontent, we must find our fulfillment in God and not seek contentment in our circumstances.

SMALL GROUP DISCUSSION GUIDE

FELLOWSHIP AND PRAYER

STARTER QUESTIONS
1. Have you ever considered that your plans for ministry might not be God's plans?
2. Can you think of times in which your worship of God was half-hearted?
3. What are some examples of good desires that can become idols?
4. When did you last tear down an idol in your own life?

SCRIPTURE TO CONSIDER
1. Read through Malachi 1. What are some indications that the people are not truly worshipping God? What is God's response? Can you think of contemporary applications of the truths in this chapter?

REVIEWING PRINCIPLES FROM THE CHAPTER
1. If you can, think through some of the conflicts in your life over the past week or month or year (situations where you have been angry, yelled, simmered with resentment, etc.). Consider other sinful fruit in your life (anxiety, worry, fear). What prompted those responses? What were you worshipping? How should you have responded? How can you seek God's help?
2. Is it possible that an aspect of orphan care ministry has become an idol in your life? How can God help you overcome idolatry?
3. How would you encourage a person to "count the cost" in caring for orphans?
4. In what ways does God equip a person for orphan care ministry?

What are the dangers of caring for the fatherless on your own strength?

5. Do you struggle with discontentment as you wait for something in your life to happen? How can your study group encourage one another to be content?

APPLICATION QUESTIONS

1. Besides those mentioned in the chapter, can you think of additional circumstances in which believers should wait before caring for orphans?

2. How could you lovingly approach a fellow believer and caution her in her ministry plans? How would you respond if someone advised you to wait to pursue a ministry you were excited about?

3. What will you do if you are unable to serve the Lord in an area of orphan care ministry that you want to? What will you do if God closes doors of opportunity?

7 The Greatness *of* Godly Affliction

In my study, on the wall facing my desk, is a framed print of Rembrandt's *Jeremiah Lamenting the Destruction of Jerusalem.* It is a sad picture. The prophet sits on a rock with a very downcast demeanor. He is looking at the ground. His head rests upon his hand. His elbow is on the collection of prophetic writings that the kings of Judah had rejected. In the background, Jerusalem is burning.

I purchased the picture during my second year of ministry to give me a sense of perspective. Things had not been going as well in my ministry as I would have liked. First, I had moved from a small church where they were just happy to have a guy doing youth ministry to a bigger church where there were greater expectations placed on the youth pastor. I felt as though I was constantly disappointing people.

Second, I was young and made a lot of the mistakes that new pastors will make. I certainly had "the seminarian swagger." The title of my candidating message was "The Pedagogy of the Church." Yeah, you read that correctly. Real heart-pounding stuff.

Third, I was a wimp. I wanted to be liked, and I wanted ministry to be easy. But it was not easy. It was downright impossible at times. I was such a wimp that it overwhelmed me when I encountered criticism from parents and, at times, other pastoral staff.

It got so bad that at one point I whisked into the senior pastor's office and told him some of my woeful story. Pastor Ritch was reading a book and seemed almost unaware of my presence. I am pretty sure he did not even look up while I was talking. I finished my tale with the words, "...and so I need to resign."

He glanced up momentarily from his book and said, "No one who looks back after putting his hand to the plow is fit for service in the kingdom of God." He then continued his reading, and I continued on in the ministry.

The picture of Jeremiah in my study reminds me that ministry is not supposed to be easy. If you use any of the contemporary rubrics by which we are apt to judge effectiveness in ministry today, Jeremiah did very poorly. There are rarely positive responses to his messages. Those who believed his prophecies were few—possibly as few as two! His influence was slight. His faithful ministry ended with the people refusing to heed his warnings and forcibly dragging him to Egypt.

Since those first few years of ministry, I have tried to develop a thicker skin, realizing that the row I have to hoe was never guaranteed to be easy. I still struggle with being a wimp. I still love ease. I do not want the ministry of Jeremiah, but I try to prepare myself for it. And in difficult circumstances, I try to rejoice as I recognize that they are beneficial for me.

John Piper's *Let the Nations Be Glad* has been one of the most influential books in shaping my philosophy of ministry. Though categorized as a missions book, it deals with themes that touch every aspect of life. For me, the most profound section of the book is the chapter on suffering. In my copy, little exclamation points litter the margins of this chapter.

It is a chapter that makes me squirm. The Scripture passages it quotes sometimes make my heart skip a beat as I consider their implications. I can still remember coming to one section of the chapter, pausing, and then rereading it several times. I knew it was right, but I had never consciously thought of life in that way before. Here's what Piper writes:

> Why does God allow this [suffering]? No, that is not quite the right question. We have to ask, Why does God appoint this? These things are part of God's plan for his people just as the suffering and death of Jesus were part of God's plan for salvation (Isa. 53:10; Acts 4:27–28). It is true that Satan can be the more immediate agent of suffering, but even he may do nothing without God's permission.
>
> Paul describes suffering as a gift of God: "It has been granted to you that for the sake of Christ you should not only believe in him but also suffer for his sake" (Phil. 1:29).
>
> Twice Peter spoke of suffering as being God's will: "It is better to suffer for doing good, if that should be God's will, than for doing evil.... Let those who suffer according to God's will entrust their souls to a faithful Creator while doing good" (1 Pet. 3:17; 4:19).[1]

This understanding of suffering is extremely rare and thoroughly biblical. God appoints his servants to suffer. It is a *gift*. The failure to embrace

---

1. Piper, *Let the Nations Be Glad*, 84.

these truths has caused the church to fail in many ways, including in her care for orphans.

Unfortunately, believers do all they can to avoid hardship and pursue the most extravagant lifestyle within their reach. If the church believed she was called to hardship, she would look profoundly different. Perhaps her members would live in smaller homes or drive older cars. Their television sets would perhaps not be quite so large. Her offering plates might be heavier as they were passed along the pews. The needs of the poor in the world would not be so profound. And, yes, the problem of the orphan would be less severe.

If God's people took it upon themselves to see difficulty in life not as something to be avoided but rather as a gift from God, we would not balk at the cost of caring for the orphan. The strain that caring for the orphan might put upon our finances or ease of life or affliction for our biological children or emotional distress would not be the obstacle to obedience it is today.

The Idolatry of Ease

Elizabeth Styffe, director of Saddleback Church's HIV/AIDS Initiative, believes that most Christians are unaware of the severity of the problem facing orphans worldwide. "Most Christians consider themselves sensitive to orphans. Statistics show that a high percentage of Christians have thought about adopting or caring for foster children. There is a reason organizations that care for orphans have large budgets. So, Christians think, 'Of course we care for the orphan.' But they have no comprehension of the scope of the need and what caring for orphans truly requires."[2] I hope she is right. The alternative is that we are aware but are unwilling to assist those in need due to our profound selfishness.

In the previous chapter, we considered the nature of idolatry and how it keeps us from pursuing our heavenly Father. An idol that is ever present in my heart is the idol of ease. I want things in my life to be as smooth as possible. I want my children not to argue. I want to have enough money to pay our bills. I want to have enough money to pay people to do the things I do not wish to do.

Worshipping the idol of ease prevents us from caring for the orphan. Michael Monroe, who helps lead a local church orphan ministry in the Dallas-Fort Worth area, sees the unwillingness of evangelicals to deal with

---

2. Elizabeth Styffe, phone conversation with author, February 18, 2010.

hard situations as a major obstacle to obedience in the area of caring for the fatherless:

> We tend to run from things that we see as being messy. We don't like messy situations. When people discuss the type of adoption they want to involve themselves in, they sometimes speak in code. We've had some couples say things like, "We'd like to adopt internationally." What they are really saying is, "An international adoption will allow us to avoid dealing with a birth mother because that would be messy."
>
> Or some couples might say, "We want a younger child." But what they are really saying is, "Older children can be messy."
>
> Or some might say, "We want to adopt from Russia or China." What they are really saying is, "We don't want to deal with the negative ethnic stereotypes that a black or brown child might have."
>
> What we see too often is that people are not wanting to confront the harsh realities of adoption. They just want a magic moment where they go to a foreign country and a little child runs to them with outstretched arms, grasps them, and says, "Thank you, Mommy, for adopting me!"
>
> What they don't realize is that when the child is handed to them, he may be biting and kicking them. Two weeks later, they will be calling us saying, "I'm having trouble attaching to my kid!" Of course they are because they went into the adoption with the wrong expectations. Adoption always involves tragedy.... Adopted children always have birth parents, whether you meet them or not![3]

Monroe is absolutely right. And many needs of precious children are not being met because we as evangelicals are worshipping the idol of ease. We are not willing to be inconvenienced for the glory of God in the life of the orphan.

Ease is an idol that diverts our attention away from the glory of God and focuses our hearts on the exaltation of self. As we exalt, our question changes from "What would God have me do to meet this need?" to "How will pursuing this ministry inconvenience me or my family?" or "How will this ministry affect my retirement planning?" or "Will this affect my ability to take the European vacation I have been longing for?"

---

3. Michael Monroe, conversation with author, November 25, 2009.

Paul, Affliction, and 2 Corinthians

Our culture is not the only one that has had an aversion to suffering. In Paul's day, there was a belief that adversity and affliction were signs of God's disfavor. The suffering that Paul had undergone was apparently one of several attacks that his critics in Corinth leveled against him.

Corinth was a large port city. It boasted two harbors, which made it a wealthy and worldly commercial center. Paul first visited the city on his second missionary journey, around A.D. 50. After he left, false teachers viciously attacked his ministry. During Paul's third missionary journey, in A.D. 55, he visited the church again. He called this a "painful visit" (2 Cor. 2:1). He was rejected by at least a vocal minority and the majority failed to support him and confront the sin in their midst.

After leaving Corinth, he wrote a "severe" letter and sent it with Titus. He was very bold in it and used his apostolic authority to call those within Corinth to repent. It was a painful letter for him to write and must have been a painful letter for the Corinthians to receive.

Paul waited in suspense, wondering how these people whom he loved so dearly would respond to what he had written. When Titus returned to him and Paul heard that they responded well, he was overjoyed, but still felt compelled to explain the reason why God had called him to such a difficult ministry. In 2 Corinthians, Paul offers an explanation for why God has his people suffer.

The Purpose of Suffering

Affliction and grief are not instruments of torture but rather a hammer and chisel in the hands of a loving God. He uses these tools in order to cause us to be made into the image he desires. Our theology of suffering must be sound and consistently applied to the ministry of orphan care.

Suffering Produces Empathy for Others

Through suffering we gain the ability to understand firsthand the suffering of others, which makes our ministry to them more effective:

> Blessed be the God and Father of our Lord Jesus Christ, the Father of mercies and God of all comfort, who comforts us in all our affliction, so that we may be able to comfort those who are in any affliction, with the comfort with which we ourselves are comforted by God. For as we share abundantly in Christ's

sufferings, so through Christ we share abundantly in comfort too. If we are afflicted, it is for your comfort and salvation; and if we are comforted, it is for your comfort, which you experience when you patiently endure the same sufferings that we suffer." (2 Cor. 1:3–6)

There are a few remarkable aspects of the empathy that is produced by suffering. First, it is God who ultimately determines what type of suffering we will endure. No difficulty we face is outside the sovereign direction of our loving, caring Father. Therefore, we are to bless him for our suffering (v. 3).

Second, notice that God grants comfort to those who are in affliction. He is blessed because of the comfort that he offers. He is called "the Father of mercies and God of all comfort" (v. 3). He "comforts us in all our affliction" (v. 4). Despite the difficult circumstances that Paul has undergone, some of which are chronicled in the rest of the epistle, Paul notes that God has brought comfort.

Third, those who have received God's comfort possess a greater ability to comfort others. Paul says that they had been comforted "so that" they would be able to "comfort those who are in any affliction" (v. 4). Paul and his companions had suffered, and now they could comfort those in Corinth.

Paul's contention is that our afflictions cause us to be better equipped to come alongside others who are suffering. Note that the goal of our comfort is not just some feel-good, "I feel your pain" type of empathy. It is an empathy that a wise God gives us so that we will be able to point those who are suffering to the sufficiency and comfort that is in Jesus Christ. It is a Christ-exalting empathy.

God calls his people to suffer afflictions as they care for orphans in order to equip them to point others to the comfort that can be found only in Christ. It is possible that God could call you to suffer grief in your life in order to allow you to point the fatherless to the "Father of mercies." It is possible that God will call you to experience great affliction as you care for a foster child so that you can point other foster parents to the cross.

I claim to teach the orphan Bible study at our church, but it might be more accurate to say that I coteach. Every time we go through the study, I ask Grace to attend the study as well. I have some pretty good material in the Bible study, but it would not be as helpful without the comments Grace adds to what I teach. She is an incredible resource and one of the reasons is because she has suffered. Her suffering causes her to be sensitive to the emotional needs of others.

When people who have gone through the Bible study are in the midst of a distressing trial, they do not usually call me. They call Grace. When a mom is struggling with understanding why she does not feel like she loves her adopted child, she calls Grace. When a couple is wrestling with a tough situation with a birth mother, they call Grace. Grace points people to the God of all comfort because she has experienced his comfort.

As you obey God's call to care for the orphan, you will face difficulty. The unrealistic vision you have of a little orphan Annie waiting for her Daddy Warbucks while singing, "Tomorrow," will be replaced with a battle-field perspective of the spiritual struggle you have been forced to engage in. And, as you receive God's comfort, you will be prepared to point your fellow soldiers to the God of all comfort.

Suffering Strengthens Our Reliance on God

As I mentioned in chapter 4, Brett and Hillary are a couple who were called by God to adopt a child who is HIV-positive. Going into the adoption, Hillary was well aware of her own inadequacies. "Some days the fear would become so intense it would almost paralyze me," she wrote. "I doubted myself, my strength, my ability, and quite often my sanity. It was then that I began to really understand God in a new way. I began to understand that God did not want someone qualified or someone gifted. He wanted me."[4] It was this perspective that would help her care for her son in God's power.

Before she was able to adopt her son, Hillary had to review his file. Early on a Saturday morning, she got into her car and drove to the foster agency. . .

> I was so excited to get the files. Excited to get to see more pic-tures of him and to learn more about him. Our caseworker told us that we needed to read the files and then let them know if we were interested in adopting him by Monday morning. I already knew we would say yes. There was never a chance in my mind that I would say no . . . until I read the files.
>
> Until I saw firsthand the horror, and let the reality of it sink in.
>
> Then, my big talk, brave attitude, devotion, save the world ideas, ran out the door—leaving me alone, crumbled, and full of FEAR.
>
> Raw fear.
> It shakes you to the core.
> Paralyzes you.
> Consumes you.

---

4. E-mail message to author, December 16, 2009.

Overcomes you.

I've had bad days like everybody else. I've experienced loss, been defeated, and felt like I had hit rock bottom. But nothing, *nothing* prepared me to look wide eyes opened at this file before me and straight into the face of evil. *Nothing.*

Two complete files, each six inches thick, with more information on this little boy's past than my heart could bear to read.

I have to admit that I am the type of person that turns off the news because I cannot stand to hear or see the evil in the world. I don't like reading the newspaper either. The news is often more than I can handle. Like many, I've become an expert at looking the other way, letting someone else take care of the dirty work. I prefer to stay in my own little world where wild flowers grow in my backyard, children swing on tire swings, and the biggest complaint in my life is the rising cost of gasoline.

So, as I opened the files and began to flip through the pages I felt myself go into shut down mode. Visibly shaken, I had to walk away. Close the files. Run. Hide—under my pillow, in a closet—anywhere. Find safety. Leave the room. Leave the horror that this little boy had lived, and just walk away. It was more than I could handle.

I didn't want to step into this pain—the real deal of what he had actually lived. I wanted to go back to my safe little world, shut the door, lock the windows, turn off the news.

My life is good, it's easy. We do not associate with that kind of evil. We don't let it become real in our lives because we run from it, hide from it. We don't let it in.

We pretend it doesn't even exist.

I began to panic. My insides were screaming, "No!" I could feel my heart beating faster and I felt my mind kick into overdrive, coming up with all sorts of good excuses to say no.

I thought of ways we could explain to people that we just *had* to say no. I thought of how we could just make a clean break, walk away . . . no, better yet *run* away as fast as we could. We could keep living our life as we knew it. Forget about this little boy. Forget he even existed. Forget that even without us he would still face this past.

And then those words that I had read just that day in my Bible came creeping into my mind. They became almost alive. Several came to mind, such as:

"But the Lord stood at my side and gave me strength." 2 Timothy 4:17.

"Trust in the Lord with all your heart, and lean not on your own understanding. In all your ways, acknowledge him and he shall direct your paths." (Proverbs 3:5–6)

"But he said to me, 'My grace is sufficient for you, for my power is made perfect in weakness.'" (2 Corinthians 12:9)

Slowly, throughout the course of the day God gave me the strength to read through the rest of the files.

God made it clear to me the *real* horror that so many children just like this sweet little boy face every day. There are children just like him all over this world, hoping for a chance. File after file of them filled with the unimaginable. We can choose to look away or we can choose to step into the pain and *be God's hands and feet.*

Later, when we finished reading the file, I shut it and looked over at my husband. With tears streaming down our faces, we held onto each other, bowed our heads, and whispered, *"Yes, Lord ... your will be done."*

By stepping into the world of evil, Brett and Hillary suffered themselves and learned about God's strength and care. Could Brett and Hillary have learned those truths regarding God's sufficiency apart from suffering? Perhaps not, for Paul tells us in 1 Corinthians 1 that it is suffering that increases our ability to rely upon God.

Of the time when Paul and his companions were in Asia, Paul writes:

We were so utterly burdened beyond our strength that we despaired of life itself. Indeed, we felt that we had received the sentence of death. But that was to make us rely not on ourselves but on God who raises the dead. He delivered us from such a deadly peril, and he will deliver us. On him we have set our hope that he will deliver us again. (2 Cor. 1:8–10)

Notice the depths to which Paul was called to suffer in Asia Minor. It got to the point that he and his companions "despaired of life itself." God's purpose behind these afflictions was to cause them to trust him more fully. As they went through difficulty, they had no choice but to rely upon God and he proved faithful. And, the more God proved faithful, the greater glory he received.

The afflictions you face when called to serve orphans will probably not be so severe that you despair of life itself, though it may be so severe that you despair of your sanity! More likely, your ministry to orphans will cause you pain in places in your heart that you were not even aware existed. As you come to a certain point, you will be forced to rely upon the only one who can help you.

Trials do not make us need God; they reveal the need that is always there. My father was diagnosed several years ago with multiple myeloma, a cancer in the bone marrow. One morning, as he discussed some of the side effects of the medication he was taking, I expressed sorrow that he was having to suffer. His response was perfect: "Don't be sorry. This has been the best year of my life. I have learned to rely upon God in a way that I would never have learned apart from the cancer. I always needed God—the cancer just revealed the depth of that need to me."

Tragedy and affliction reveal the ever-present need we have for God's grace. Unfortunately, many believers are so reluctant to undergo suffering that they never get to experience the greatness of God's provision. There are aspects of God's goodness that they are never able to taste.

Suffering Proclaims the Power of God

Suffering has external effects as well. Afflictions proclaim the power of God to the people around us. In 2 Corinthians 4:7, Paul presents this truth in a metaphor: "we have this treasure in jars of clay, to show that the surpassing power belongs to God and not to us." Jars of clay have little intrinsic value, but if they contain treasure then they become very valuable indeed. Suffering highlights our inabilities and God's limitless capabilities.

Our purpose is not to display the greatness of ourselves but the treasure within. The power of God allows us, the jars of clay, to exhibit power beyond human expectation, *and few things display the greatness of the treasure within more than suffering.* Paul contrasts what they have experienced with how they have been able to persevere due to God's power: "We are afflicted in every way, but not crushed; perplexed, but not driven to despair; persecuted, but not forsaken; struck down, but not destroyed; always carrying in the body the death of Jesus, so that the life of Jesus may also be manifested in our bodies" (vv. 8–10).

Suffering is accompanied by the manifestation of God's power in the midst of that suffering: "For we who live are always being given over to death for Jesus' sake, so that the life of Jesus also may be manifested in our mortal flesh. So death is at work in us, but life in you" (vv. 11–12).

In other words, the fact that we undergo suffering and bear up under it proclaims the life of Christ within us. One of the reasons that God appoints suffering for his saints is so that they can proclaim his gospel. The church's willingness to undertake the arduous task of ministering to the fatherless is a powerful witness. Dr. Mark Tatlock, senior vice president and provost at Master's College, observes that in "every era of church history, it was the church who championed the cause of the widows and orphans. The world rightly accuses the church of hypocrisy when we proclaim a message of peace and reconciliation and there is no visible expression of it. Compassion ministries validate the gospel."[5]

Andy Lehman, vice-president of Lifesong for Orphans, concurs. "Orphan care ministry proclaims to the world that the church is willing to meet tangible needs. The ultimate goal of the church is not to be seen as relevant by the world. However, an outgrowth of the orphan ministry can be relevancy as it is seen that the church meets some practical needs."[6] Meeting needs and doing "good deeds" can be used by the Holy Spirit to soften hearts and make them more receptive to the gospel.

Elizabeth Styffe tells the heartbreaking story of a young man who was an orphan in Rwanda and converted to Islam. When the local Christian pastor asked him why, he said that some Muslims had approached him, opened the Christian Bible, and showed him James 1:27: "Religion that is pure and undefiled before God, the Father, is this: to visit orphans and widows in their affliction, and to keep oneself unstained from the world." "We take care of orphans," they told him. "Your Christian friends do not. Therefore, we are the pure and true religion." The young man agreed that the Christians had not cared for him. He told the church that they did not have the true religion. The church was condemned by its own Scriptures. Today, the church has repented and has a ministry to orphans.

Suffering Yields Great Rewards

As we suffer, we invest in eternal glory with the currency of pain.

So we do not lose heart. Though our outer self is wasting away, our inner self is being renewed day by day. For this light momentary affliction is preparing for us an eternal weight of glory beyond all comparison, as we look not to the things that are seen but to the things that are unseen. For the things that are seen are transient, but the things that are unseen are eternal. (2 Cor. 4:16–18)

Those who suffer in the flesh in a godly manner are preparing for a

---

5. Mark Tatlock, phone conversation with author, March 9, 2010.
6. Andy Lehman, conversation with author, November 20, 2009.

reward that is beyond comprehension. No matter how much caring for orphans costs you, as you invest in affliction by God's grace, you will reap glory that renders the cost insignificant.

Radical changes have taken place in our daughter's life and demeanor since we brought her home from the orphanage. These changes did not come cheaply. There have been many long days and nights spent with her. There have been things that we did not do so that we could focus our attention on sweet Ellie. And the fruit has been enormous. Today at lunch, she was asking me to look at something and said, "Look at this, Daaadddyyy!" I laughed at her and told her to say my name again. Seeing this girl who had been frightened and overwhelmed by life now joyfully call out her daddy's name makes my heart sing.

There was momentary affliction but even the temporal gains have made it worthwhile. I am floored at the thought of the eternal joy we will experience as the result of some momentary affliction.

Suffering Results in Greater Humility

There is tremendous shame associated with being a "bad" parent. Parenting conferences at our church are usually well-attended, and no one wants to be seen as the parent who is doing a poor job shepherding their child's heart. Maybe being a pastor makes me particularly sensitive to this and I cringe when I hear the phrase "pastor's kid" even jokingly bantered about. Knowing that pride is at the root of my sensitivity, I try to practice humble transparency, openly admitting my faults as a parent where appropriate in my ministry.

It's not that I have much of a choice. My children struggle with the same sin nature that I still battle, and at times sinful behavior manifests itself publicly. The truth—as hard as it is to admit—is that I am not the ideal parent. The struggles I have had as a parent are glaring reminders of my insufficiencies—and that is a good thing. Hard, difficult circumstances teach me about my inabilities and humble me.

Suffering results in greater humility. Paul explains to the Corinthians that he received revelations that were of such surpassing worth that it might have been tempting to boast:

> So to keep me from becoming conceited because of the surpassing greatness of the revelations, a thorn was given me in the flesh, a messenger of Satan to harass me, to keep me from being conceited. Three times I pleaded with the Lord about this, that it should leave me. But he said to me, "My grace is sufficient for you, for my power is made perfect in weakness." Therefore I will boast

all the more gladly of my weaknesses, so that the power of Christ may rest upon me. (2 Cor. 12:7–9)

The "thorn" of suffering reminds Paul not to exalt himself but instead to depend upon God's grace.

Churches Avoid Suffering

Worship of ease is not a malady that affects individuals only. Churches also go to great lengths to avoid putting themselves in places where they may be uncomfortable. Churches are sometimes so concerned with their own glory, prestige, and comfort that they are tempted to direct their resources to ministries that will glorify their own kingdoms instead of Christ's.

Orphans do not tithe well. They are not in prominent positions where they can promote the greatness of your church. Ministry to them requires having a right understanding of the church's role and a willingness to embrace that so God's grace will be increased.

The Joy of Doing Difficult Things

The remarkable thing about those who have done hard things with a God-centered focus is that they possess great joy as a result of their suffering. As you talk with people who have been through grueling circumstances, you find that they are glad they went through them. My friend Jack Kragt is an adoptive father of two girls from China. A passionate advocate for adoption, he was instrumental in getting this book published. As I was corresponding with him regarding the subject matter of this book, he mentioned the pain that he and his wife had gone through:

Incidentally, let me share with you one sentence that I often share with those who are considering adopting or in the horrible pains of a failed pregnancy. This sentence is profound, true, but very difficult for those considering adoption and those in the middle of failed in vitro to comprehend. The line I often state is that "Sometimes God's very best child for you is not a biological child, but an adopted child." I often tell them how glad I am that my wife and I never had biological children because I am not convinced that I would have adopted additional children if we had biological children. Yet, I would have missed the two greatest blessings in my life, and I still cannot comprehend two better children for me than my two.

It is interesting that those who have used their time of suffering wisely have seen God's greater plan at work through terrible circumstances. They would not trade their time of testing for any worldly treasure you could offer. Suffering is the gift of a loving God

SMALL GROUP DISCUSSION GUIDE

FELLOWSHIP AND PRAYER

STARTER QUESTIONS
1. What are some times of suffering the Lord has brought you through? How did he use them in your life?
2. How are you sometimes tempted to value ease instead of God?

SCRIPTURE TO CONSIDER
As you review the principles from the chapter in questions 2–6 below, read the passages from 2 Corinthians that correspond to each section.

REVIEWING PRINCIPLES FROM THE CHAPTER
1. What is your attitude toward suffering? In what ways is it similar to the attitude of the Corinthians?
2. How does suffering produce empathy (2 Cor. 1:3–6)? Can you think of some ways that God has used suffering in your life to produce empathy for others?
3. How does suffering strengthen your reliance upon God (2 Cor. 1:8–10)?
4. How is the power of God proclaimed through suffering (2 Cor. 4:7–10)? Have you or your church had the opportunity to share the power of the gospel through difficult times or by caring for orphans?
5. Is the thought of God's future reward exciting to you (2 Cor. 4:16–19)? Why does God want us to be motivated by future rewards? Is that selfish? What are the rewards he offers us?
6. Are there ways in which suffering has humbled you (2 Cor. 12:7–10)? How does this better prepare you to care for the orphan?

APPLICATION QUESTIONS

1. Does the thought of suffering make you nervous? In what tangible ways can we prepare ourselves for suffering?
2. Can you think of ways God might call you to suffer as you care for the orphan?
3. How can you help those who are currently going through trying circumstances?

8 Decision Making *in* Orphan Care Ministry

*W*hen *I announced my engagement* to a friend who was a pastor, his response was not exactly romantic.

"That's great," he said. "I'm glad you guys are getting married."

He paused.

"Of course, we make getting married too hard."

I agreed, thinking that he was talking about the lengthy (and expensive) courtship, the romantic (and expensive) proposal, and the elaborate (and expensive) wedding.

But that wasn't what he meant. "We make too big of a show about picking the 'right' man or woman to marry and trying to determine God's will in the whole process. Why, I'm convinced that I could line up ten girls in my office right now who were all committed to the Lord and you could pick any one of them and be just fine."

I tried to envision such a scenario in my mind. I admitted that having a line-up to choose from would have saved a lot of time, but my guess was that the young ladies would have objected to the process. Also, I liked to think that Whitney would have protested the arrangement.

When I shared his theory with Whitney, I was glad to find that she did indeed think it was lacking. She proceeded to lay out the reasons that she believed God had planned to bring us together. She believed—and time has proven her correct—that God had prepared ministry for us to do that was uniquely designed for us as a team.

My friend was attempting to argue against a view of God's will that paralyzes people with fear that they will make a wrong decision. Sometimes we agonize about decisions we need to make and try to find direction when God has not given us any explicit directions. We are like the lovelorn young man in the 1966 Lovin' Spoonfuls song "Did You Ever Have to Make Up Your Mind," who "really digs" a girl and then gets "distracted by her older sister." He then faces a painful choice. He must "say yes to one and let the other one ride." Throughout the song, he seems completely overwhelmed by the difficult decisions he must make.

The lovelorn, of course, are not the only ones who must make difficult decisions. Anyone involved in caring for the fatherless knows that there is sometimes great anguish in discerning God's calling and direction. For example, couples who are considering adoption face a legion of questions concerning God's leading: Where do we adopt from? What "kind" of child do we adopt? What needs should we be willing to meet? Is it OK to have a preference for a boy or a girl? Their anguish often stems from the fear of making the wrong decision. The cry of couples in these circumstances has at its heart an important question: How can I know what "God's will" is in this circumstance?

As I talk with people about decisions they must make and with pastors and theologians regarding how to discern God's leading, I find we tend to err in one of two primary ways. Sometimes, we become obsessed with finding "God's will" and resort to some creative and unbiblical means to find it. We fail to realize that God has not always given us specific instructions in a given situation. I'll elaborate on this more in the following pages.

The other error, however, is to downplay the reality that God directs our steps. We sometimes fail to acknowledge that we serve a sovereign God who holds in his hand every moment of our day and, therefore, God has a very specific plan for our lives. Even though God has not promised to give us divine guidance in every situation, we have confidence that through prayer and the enabling of his Holy Spirit, we are in his care as we are obedient to his revealed will for us.

The Fear of Making the Wrong Decision

There are numerous understandings of decision making in the evangelical camp, and I will not be able to fully resolve their differences. My aim in this chapter is more modest. I want to address those aspects of God's will that are most relevant to decision making in orphan care ministry.

Debunking Ishmael Theology

There have been several times when talking with believers about life in general and orphan care ministry specifically that they have brought up the story of Ishmael. Imagine how you might respond in the following fictional scenario.

Roger is considering adopting a child. As you talk about the process of adopting, he mentions that he and his wife are struggling to decide between international and domestic adoption.

"This is a big deal," Roger laments. "There are so many decisions we need to make. In fact, each decision just seems to lead to more choices. I don't want to make a mistake." He thinks for a moment, as if he's not sure how to articulate his frustration.

"After all," he confides, "I don't want to create an Ishmael. Abraham failed to trust God to provide him with the son he had promised through his wife Sarah. So Abraham worked to bring about a son on his own terms and fathered Ishmael with Sarah's servant Hagar. I want to wait for the Lord's will, for Isaac instead of Ishmael."

Roger is concerned that if he fails to figure out God's plan for his life, he might end up with a child whom God did not intend for their family. He fears that if through his sin he ends up with the wrong child, his family will be permanently out of God's will. If Roger is correct in his thinking, he faces a tremendous problem and, what is worse, he has no special revelation to help him make sure that he gets the right child.

The more I mull over "Ishmael theology," the more concerned I become with its implications for orphan care ministry. Ishmael theology holds that God has one child in mind for Roger and there is a possibility that he could wind up with the wrong one if he doesn't figure out which one it is! If he fails to follow God in perfect obedience, Roger could wind up with a second-rate child instead of God's best. If Ishmael theology were true, we would need to make sure we picked the exact right agency, the exact right country, the exact right referral, and so on.

Ishmael theology contains several misconceptions regarding decision making and orphan care. First, Ishmael theology teaches that God not only has a detailed, specific plan for our care for orphans but that his plan can and must be discerned with perfect clarity. Second, Ishmael theology teaches that God's detailed, sovereign plan for orphans and for ourselves can be thwarted by our disobedience. Third, Ishmael theology teaches that we may wind up caring for a child that was not God's best plan for us because we did not discover God's secret will. All of these are false.

Roger's application of the story of Ishmael does not mesh with the biblical account. Certainly there were consequences for Abraham's failure to believe God, but the product of his union with Hagar—Ishmael—was not the punishment. God did not view the life of Ishmael as second-rate. His life was not outside of God's will—nor are the lives of all of his descendants!

God shows care and concern for this child who came from less than ideal circumstances. He himself names the child Ishmael, which means "God hears," telling Hagar when she is pregnant, "You shall call his name Ishmael, because the LORD has listened to your affliction" (Gen. 16:11). When Hagar and Ishmael are sent away, God intervenes and protects them (Gen. 21:8–21).

It is true that Abraham and Sarah failed to trust in God's timing to bring about his revealed will and that sin had consequences. But unless God has given you specific revelation concerning how to care for the orphan, looking to the story of Ishmael to create a sense of fear that you might get the "wrong child" is missing the point of the story of Isaac and missing Scripture's other teachings regarding the will of God.

In this chapter, we will think through how Scripture describes God's plan for our lives. My goal is not to attack those who hold to a different understanding of God's will, but rather to encourage you to have freedom and joy as you seek to follow God in obedience.[1] Either trying to wait until you perceive God's specific will with absolute clarity or worrying that you may miss God's exact, perfect plan will cause undue worry and frustration because that is not how God told us to live. As we conclude the chapter, we will also consider principles to help us apply God's revealed will to making decisions and to give us confidence that we are acting in obedience to him.

Where There's a Will

Depending on context, the phrase "God's will," as it is used in Scripture and in our daily lives, can have various meanings. We will briefly consider the *decreed* will of God, the *desired* will of God, and the *directional* will of God.[2]

The Decreed Will of God

One aspect of God's will in Scripture is what theologians call his "decreed will." This is also sometimes called his "secret will" because God's plans are generally unknown before they occur. Wayne Grudem defines this aspect of God's will as that which "includes his hidden decrees by which he governs the universe and determines everything that will happen."[3]

There are several things Scripture tells us about this aspect of God's will. For example, we know that whatever God decrees will certainly come about. His ability to fulfill his plans is proof of his deity. God says to "remember the former things of old; for I am God, and there is no other;

---

1. For other evangelical understandings of God's will, see Huffman, *How Then Should We Choose*.
2. These aspects of God's will are given different terms by various theologians. I am employing the terms used by Kevin DeYoung in his short book on the subject of God's will, *Just Do Something*, 17–26.
3. Grudem, *Systematic Theology*, 213.

I am God, and there is none like me, declaring the end from the beginning and from ancient times things not yet done, saying, 'My counsel shall stand, and I will accomplish all my purpose" (Isa. 46:9–10). Whatever God decides to do, he does.

Because we do not know God's secret will, we must hold our plans tentatively. When Paul talks of travelling to Corinth, he writes to the church, "I will come to you soon, if the Lord wills" (1 Cor. 4:19). In Romans, he is referring to God's secret will when he says that he is "asking that somehow by God's will I may now at last succeed in coming to you" (Rom. 1:10; cf. 15:32). James says those who speak confidently of what tomorrow brings "boast" and that "all such boasting is evil" (James 4:16).

There should be great humility, therefore, when a person speaks of a certain course of action they are planning as being "in God's will." As we think about caring for orphans, we do not know what God's plan is with clarity. We can sense his leading and trust his care, but we should be very careful not to adamantly or arrogantly presume to know his thinking. The plan for our lives is held in the Lord's hand and not our own.

The Desired Will of God

The word "will" is also used to describe God's instructions to humanity. This is his "desired" or "revealed" will for believers. Wayne Grudem writes: "God's revealed will is sometimes also called God's *will of precept* or will of command. This revealed will of God is God's declared will concerning *what we should do* or what God *commands* us to do."[4]

When Scripture commands believers to be obedient to God's will, it is speaking of being in conformity to his declared moral will—what he desires us to do. Christ is speaking of the desired will of God when he declares, "Behold I have come to do your will, O God" (Heb. 10:7). Paul urges believers to "discern what is the will of God" and defines that will as a moral will—that which "is good and acceptable and perfect" (Rom. 12:2). The will of God is accomplished as believers worship God through their moral conduct.

The Directional Will of God

The third meaning of the phrase "God's will" relates to how God directs individuals' *specific decisions*. For example, we know that God's will is for us to care for the orphan. This is his decreed will. It is clear and absolute. But what do you do when you are trying to narrow down which country you are planning to adopt from? When believers use the phrase

---

4. Ibid., emphasis in the original.

"God's will," they usually mean *how can I discern God's hidden plan for this specific situation in which there is no biblical guidance?* What I find interesting is that Scripture never uses the phrase "God's will" in this manner.

The Wily Will of God

Many Christians view God's will as a narrow path, shrouded in a mysterious mist, that winds along the edge of a cliff. One false step and we careen into the abyss forever ...

Fear of Falling off the Path

In *How Then Should We Choose: Three Views on God's Will and Decision Making*, Henry Blackaby and his son Richard Blackaby present a view of God's will called "The Specific-Will View." The term "specific will" can be somewhat misleading because many Christians would agree that God has a specific will or plan. The Blackabys use the term to argue that God has a specific plan for each person *and that it can be consistently discerned.* Furthermore, this view contends that trouble results when we deviate from that path.

The Blackabys give an illustration in their chapter of a young man named Joe. Joe is a committed believer who becomes infatuated with Nancy, a nominal believer:

> Though professing to be a Christian, she is weak and unstable in her faith. They might marry with feelings of love for one another. But when Joe begins the process of preparing for his calling, he will discover his wife is reluctant to make the necessary sacrifices. Not feeling any sense of call to ministry herself, Nancy only wants her husband to get a job so they can afford to purchase their first house and start a family. When Joe becomes involved in ministry activities, Nancy grows jealous of the time he gives to the church. Ultimately Joe could end up surrendering his efforts to become a pastor and live the rest of his life wondering what might have been if he had been supported in his call to the ministry.[5]

The inference seems to be that if Joe married Nancy, he would be operating under God's plan B, having missed out on God's ideal plan A.

Let us not minimize the reality of the consequences of poor decision making, but the scenario above leads to some troubling conclusions. While

---

5. Huffman, *How Then Should We Choose*, 78.

the Blackabys acknowledge that God has a (new?) perfect will for a person no matter what has happened in the past, the unavoidable inference is that once we have sinned and deviated from the path, we spend the rest of our lives outside of God's original, perfect will. Joe will never be able to get back on that path because he has imprisoned himself in a second-rate marriage. Can you imagine the sweet anniversary cards Joe could write to Nancy: "I love you because God says to even though both he and I know you were a BIG mistake."

Staying on the Path Through Hocus-Pocus

This understanding of God's will is not a biblical one, and the fears it spawns are unbiblical as well. Through the ages, pagans have attempted to find out what their gods wanted them to do through a variety of ways, such as divination, astrology, dreams, or reading livers. Believers sometimes have a similar view of attempting to find God's will, looking for special extrabiblical signs to point them to God's specific will. Bruce Waltke writes, "When I hear Christians talking about the will of God, they often use phrases such as 'If only I could find God's will,' as though he is keeping it hidden from them, or 'I'm praying that I'll discover his will for my life,' because they apparently believe the Lord doesn't want them to find it or that he wants to make it as hard as possible for them to find it so that they will prove their worth."[6] This understanding of God's will is not biblical.

Penetrating the Mist

As I critique this understanding of God's will, let me be clear about what I am *not* saying. I am not saying that God does not lead us in the specific decisions we make. Clearly, Scripture tells us that prayer and the Holy Spirit, for example, help guide us. As we live our lives and make decisions in accordance with Scripture, we can trust that God is still directing us, even in areas where we can't discern his leading.

My criticism is specifically directed at the expectation that we can and must discern his leading perfectly beforehand. There are numerous reasons to critique the view that God's will is some sort of magical riddle to be solved. First, and most importantly, "the New Testament gives no explicit command to 'find God's will,' nor can you find any particular instruction on how to go about finding God's will."[7]

Second, this understanding of God's will is illogical. James MacDonald

---

6. Waltke, *Finding the Will of God*, 7.
7. Ibid., 12.

illustrates the absurdity of this view of God's will as he considers its application to marriage:

> If there's only one perfect, lifetime partner in God's will, and you have to find that person, what happens if you make the wrong choice? I mean if there's only one possible right choice, it's conceivable that some of us will make the wrong choice, right? And what happens if you make the wrong choice? And then, God forbid—you have kids. Those kids were never supposed to exist. So now the person you were supposed to marry is married to someone else and they're having kids that were never supposed to exist.... Now those kids are all grown up. They've got nobody to marry—they're not even supposed to be here....The whole thing is ludicrous. In a generation or two, God's perfect will would be a memory. The arrangement doesn't make sense, but people try to live their lives this way.[8]

My belief is that Ellie was planned for our family before the beginning of time, but I had no way of knowing that for certain before we began to act. We acted in obedience to God's revealed word, trusting him with the circumstances we could not see.

What I think comes across clearly in MacDonald's scenario is the absurdity of believing that God's perfect will for our lives is so easily thwarted. If every time someone violated God's desired will it resulted in a situation outside of his perfect will, there would be profound implications for orphan care ministry. Something has already occurred that is at odds with God's desired will that caused a child to become an orphan. Perhaps a child was born out of wedlock or the mother was unable to care for the child due to someone else's sin. The very existence of orphans in the world is a flagrant violation of God's desired will.

If you insist on assuming personal responsibility for achieving God's "perfect will," caring for orphans will be a difficult ministry for you. Orphan care is messy, and those who are involved in it are picking up the damaged pieces of shipwrecked lives. If God had only one plan for every person's life that could be tumbled out of through disobedience, our situation—and the situation of orphans—would be rather hopeless. How much more helpful it is to see God's will as a beautiful tapestry that includes even sinful decisions!

Third, even if this understanding of God's perfect will were logical, it

---

8. MacDonald, *The Way of Wisdom*, 43.

is hopelessly impractical. There is no way to implement it consistently in our task of making decisions. For the specific-will view to be correct, it would mean that God must always provide specific direction in every situation. Our hopeless task would be to figure out what that direction was. Recognizing God's speech becomes hopelessly subjective and speculative when not tied to the clear revelation of Scripture.[9]

The problem with using circumstances as an arbiter in discerning God's will is that we cherry-pick the evidence. Let us pretend that you are having trouble deciding where to adopt from. You and your wife are at a Chinese buffet and talking about how to make a decision. While discussing your conundrum, you see a couple from church who just adopted a child from China. After dinner, you open up a fortune cookie that says, "Future decision will go well" on one side and "Made in China" on the other. You both come to the conclusion that this must mean that God wants you to adopt from China, but what happens if you get indigestion later that night? Is that God telling you to avoid China? What if the couple you met at the restaurant leave your church amid contentious circumstances? What is God trying to reveal then? In short, the problem with making decisions based upon your circumstances is that it is impossible to know for certain what they are telling you.

Rightly Understanding Decision Making

There are several principles we can glean from God's Word concerning his will and how it interacts with the decisions we make.

God Is Sovereign and Has a Plan

We must affirm that God does indeed have a sovereign and specific plan for our lives. Sometimes in our desire to emphasize the fact that we cannot base our decisions on discerning what his specific course for our lives is, we fail to simultaneously emphasize that his sovereign plan for our lives encompasses every detail. This is of immense comfort when we find ourselves in a difficult situation in caring for orphans. When a child is spitting in our face and telling us that he hates us, we do not need to question whether or not God is aware of what is happening. We did not make some mistake that caused us to be in this alternate universe where things are bad.

---

9. The Blackabys themselves seem to tacitly acknowledge this problem. "The key to knowing God's will is being able to recognize when He is speaking to you" (Huffman, *How Then Should We Choose*, 53).

In fact, suffering, as we saw in the previous chapter, is part of his plan for our lives. We can have confidence that we are in his ordained plan for our lives.

God's Plan Is Largely Secret

We must also accept that God's sovereign will is largely secret. We do not know what tomorrow has in store, nor even the next moment. The psalmist in Psalm 31 faces some dire circumstances, and from an outsider's perspective, it would appear that God has deserted him. But the psalmist responds differently, showing us that sometimes the reason God may choose to withhold knowledge of the future from us is to cause us to rely more fully upon him. The psalmist tells God, "But I trust in you, O Lord; I say, 'You are my God.' *My times are in your hand*; rescue me from the hand of my enemies and from my persecutors!" (Ps. 31:14–15, emphasis added).

God Does Not Command Us to Discern His Specific Will

We are not instructed by God to discern his specific will. Since even small events are planned and governed by God, many make the inference that we need to try to find what his plan is. In his wisdom, God has chosen not to reveal the specifics of his plan to us (Deut. 29:29). God's word has given us all that we need pertaining to life and godliness (2 Peter 1:3). If it were crucial for us to be able to discern what decision God would have us make in every situation, he could have provided us guidance for how to do so.

God Directs His Children

This does not mean God is not concerned with the decisions we make or that he leaves us to our own devices as we traverse the world. I believe that he provides guidance through prayer, circumstances, and the leading of the Holy Spirit. This guidance does not provide us with certainty that we have found his hidden will, but rather gives us confidence that the decisions we make are within his plan for our lives.

We Must Conform to God's Moral Will

God provides direction to his children through the moral imperatives in Scripture, which we obey through the Holy Spirit's enabling. This is the primary focus of God's will in Scripture. Frankly, I often find that I have a much greater need to be obedient in the big areas of life than I need direction in the little areas. I suspect this is true with most of us. Before we begin to worry about those areas in which God is less clear, we should probably focus on those areas in which he has spoken with breathtaking clarity!

Imagine a man standing at a new car dealership looking at two new sports cars. "Lord," he prays, "please give me a sign as to whether I should choose the blue car or the yellow car." But as this man waits for a sign from God—perhaps an inner voice or maybe even a Herbie-like beep of the horn—there is more going on in his life. This man is currently in a great deal of debt, much of which is due to some very poor financial decisions. He has a love for the things of this world and it has expressed itself in covetousness. His family has not given to their church in months. He is working lots of extra hours in order to keep current with payments. The long hours have kept him away from his family. When he is home, he is a very angry man, and he blames the pressures of work for his anger.

In reality, God's revealed will to this man shows that what he needs is not help picking between a blue or yellow car. He needs to get off the car lot and divest himself of the things of this world. Far too often, when we are seeking God's will, we are not truly asking what God wants us to do; we are asking God to help us make a decision between two roads that are both wrong.

Scripture Provides Guidance for Complete Obedience

God has provided Scripture for every circumstance in which we find ourselves. As we have already seen, there are many explicit commands that inform our decision making. Simply following these commands considerably narrows the choices available to us.

Even where there are no explicit commands, Scripture informs our decision-making process. For example, the Bible calls us to be wise and tells us how wisdom can be found. In its pages we find that wisdom begins with fearing God (Prov. 1:7). We learn that there is wisdom in the aged (Job 12:12). We find that wisdom is in many counselors (Prov. 15:22; cf., Prov. 12:15).

Scripture also teaches us how to be led by the Spirit. In Galatians 5:22–23, we learn how to examine our conduct to see if we are producing the fruit of the Spirit. When our choices are not characterized by love, joy, peace, patience, kindness, goodness, faithfulness, gentleness, or self-control, we are not spirit-filled, which is a violation of God's moral will (Eph. 5:18).

If a believer is following Scripture's guidance, she need not fear that she is missing a hidden sign. If there is an area in which no clear guidance is given, as she follows God's desired will in other areas and commits unclear areas to the Lord in prayer, she can be confident that she is proceeding in obedience.

God Calls His Children to Press On

When we have disobeyed God's revealed will, God calls us to repent and move forward. Paul had engaged in vicious, systematic persecution of Christ's church. If anyone ever fell out of God's will for their life, surely it was Paul. Some might have thought that he should live the rest of his life wallowing in guilt and remorse, but Paul came to a different conclusion. "Forgetting what lies behind," he wrote to the church at Philippi, "and straining forward to what lies ahead, I press on toward the goal for the prize of the upward call of God in Christ Jesus" (Philippians 3:13–14). Many of us would like to have do-overs, but there is no restart button in life. God says to press on.

I heard a story on the radio of a woman who, at the end of her life, was disappointed that she had never pursued her "one true love." After they had both married others, she wished that she had made a different decision. The point of the story was supposed to be that we should follow our dreams, but I took away a different moral: we should be content with what God has provided. Her problem was not that she had missed God's plan for her life but that she had a heart of discontentment. There is a distinct possibility that this woman would have been pining over whichever man she didn't marry because of her lack of satisfaction with God's blessings. There is something fundamentally wrong with us when we dwell on what-might-have-been. It demonstrates a lack of trust in God.

Circumstances Are Not Predictive, But May Be Descriptive

Finally, although circumstances are not predictive of God's plans for our future, they can clearly reveal his present and past will. There are some situations that reveal God's will because they close doors. When the elders at my church explicitly give me an instruction that is not contrary to God's Word, I am confident that I need to obey it. I can also look at past circumstances and realize—to some degree—what God's plan for me was. I have full confidence that it was God's will for me to marry Whitney, have children, and work at Bethany Community Church. Why? Because that's what happened.

God's Will and the Orphan

I had thought about entitling this chapter: "Red, Brown, Yellow, Black, or White? How to Decide Which One Is Right." All this abstract talk of how God's will works is fine, you say, but I still have to make a decision by Friday about what country to adopt from. And I need to check "male" or "female" on this paperwork and I don't know what to do! And I know I'm called to give financially to care for orphans, but should I give to a couple who is pursuing adoption or to an orphanage?

I have a confession to make. I don't know what you should do, but before you throw this book across the room in frustration, I do have some suggestions for you as you make a decision on how to care for the orphan.

Search God's Word

The first task is to search God's Word. As you do so, you will notice those areas in which his moral will is clearly revealed. Have you begun to take steps of obedience in caring for orphans? Read through the principles in this book and the supporting Scripture. Make sure you understand God's revealed moral will concerning the orphan.

As you do this, examine the motives of your heart. Scripture warns us that our hearts are incredibly wicked and prone to lead us astray when making decisions. It is possible that you may feel "called" to not follow God in obedience because that path seems too painful or too difficult. A path's degree of difficulty should not be what determines our course.

This also means considering the leading and the fruit of the Spirit in your life. In Ephesians, Paul instructs us not to be foolish, but rather "understand what the will of the Lord is. And do not get drunk with wine, for that is debauchery, but be filled with the Spirit" (5:17–18). It is clearly God's will that we be filled with his Spirit. In Galatians, God lays out the characteristics of one who is living under the flesh and contrasts these with the fruit of the Spirit: "But the fruit of the Spirit is love, joy, peace, patience, kindness, goodness, faithfulness, gentleness, self-control; against such things there is no law" (Gal. 5:22–23). A good way to test whether or not you are being obedient to God—being controlled by the Spirit—is whether you are manifesting the fruit of the Spirit in your life.

Seek Counsel from Godly People

Second, seek wise counsel from others. "Without counsel plans fail, but with many advisers they succeed" (Prov. 15:22). There are going to be insights and guidance that others can offer you as they hear about your plans. Often, our tendency is to seek out counsel in order to have our own opinions validated instead of having them honestly evaluated.

It is entirely possible you will need to hear some difficult things from family, friends, or spiritual leaders as you consider caring for orphans. Some counsel you will need to reject and other counsel weigh carefully. You and your church leadership may have different understandings of how you should proceed in beginning the ministry. Your responsibility is to graciously and gratefully receive the counsel of others.

Pray for God's Leading

Third, beseech the Lord to direct your steps. All of the decisions that we make should be made with prayer. But for what are we praying? A mystical sign? A breeze that whispers what we should do?

As we pray, one of the most crucial things we are asking for is that God would deepen our understanding of his revealed will and grant us the wisdom to apply it to our circumstances. Paul prays that the Ephesians would be given "a spirit of wisdom and of revelation in the knowledge of him" (Eph. 1:17). We are also praying that we would be able to follow his moral will. Paul asks that God would strengthen believers so that Christ can indwell them and they can be filled with the fullness of God (Eph. 3:14–19). We are praying that he would work in circumstances to allow us to pursue a path of ministry (Rom. 15:30–32). We are praying that he would work in the hearts of others (1 Tim. 2:1–2).

Sometimes, after praying about a decision, you may feel a great sense of confidence in pursuing a certain course of action. This does not mean, however, that we can use our prayers as evidence that we are right and others wrong about what decisions should be made. You may be tempted to say things like, "God has told me that our church needs to do such and such." I would avoid claiming that God has told you to do anything unless you are referring to a clear directive from Scripture." So, for example, I can say that God has told me that I need to love my wife, but I can't say that God has told me to buy her a diamond ring.

It is better to see prayer as a request for God to guide our footsteps. We are asking for him to help us apply Scripture and confirm in our hearts the path we are following. We are trusting that, as we are being obedient to God's moral will, we are not sinning as we make decisions in areas that are not explicitly covered in Scripture.

Submit to God's Will in Your Circumstances

Fourth, submit to God's revealed will in circumstances as you care for orphans. In Philippians 4, Paul expresses his confidence in God even in the midst of trials:

> I have learned in whatever situation I am to be content. I know how to be brought low, and I know how to abound. In any and every circumstance, I have learned the secret of facing plenty

and hunger, abundance and need. I can do all things through him who strengthens me. . . . And my God will supply every need of yours according to his riches in glory in Christ Jesus." (vv. 11–13, 19)

When confronted with circumstances that are less than ideal, Paul responds with contentment, trusting God to supply his needs. As we care for orphans, you and I must submit to God as his plans sometimes prove to be different than our own.

Joyfully Make a Decision

Fifth, joyfully make a decision! Do not become so paralyzed with indecision that you cannot move forward when God is calling. Mike and Rachel are a couple in our church who have joyfully engaged in the ministry of caring for an orphan. In 2004, they became parents for the first time with the birth of a beautiful little girl. Shortly thereafter, they decided to try to expand their family. They suffered two miscarriages and, in 2006, they learned that a medical condition made recurring miscarriages likely. Due to the possibility of having another miscarriage, Mike and Rachel decided that they would not continue to try to have biological children. The same week that they learned of their condition, our church announced the beginning of the orphan ministry.

The first event was an informational meeting. God's care for the orphan and the way that the church was called by God to come alongside families were presented. At the meeting, it was shown that there were a variety of ways available to care for the orphan: foster care, prayer team, financial support, mentoring, adoption, and so on. "Attending that meeting, we were both blessed by hearing adoption described as a way to change a child's heart and life forever," Rachel later told me.

Following the informational meeting, we had Mike and Rachel over to our house. We asked them how they thought God might be leading them as they considered caring for the orphan. Naturally cautious and careful people, they responded that they were still mulling over their options. After they left, Whitney and I concluded that if they did consider orphan care, it would be a long process before they determined how they would minister.

Imagine our surprise when, just a few days later, we saw them again and found not only that they had decided to adopt but that they had picked an out-of-country adoption and had already turned in their application. The following year was a whirlwind of activity. Rachel's father was very ill, and in his graciousness, God allowed little Steven to come home in time to meet his new grandfather.

Notice how Mike and Rachel made their decision. Their circumstances were certainly used by God to help them look at his Word more closely, but their decision was not based upon situational revelation. They did not say that because the orphan ministry began at the same time they found out about their medical condition God was absolutely telling them to adopt. God closed the door on one situation, and Mike and Rachel had the freedom to pursue a different avenue while trusting his leading.

Let us consider just a few of the options our friends had after finding out about their medical condition and the orphan care ministry. First, they could have decided to do nothing. Clearly, this would be wrong, not because of their circumstances but because of what God's Word teaches. Second, they could have become angry and frustrated that they could not have a child and chosen to pursue adoption as a means of satisfying an idol. Here, they would have been doing a good thing, but with wrong motives. Third, after examining God's Word, they could have decided that God was calling them to care for the orphan. This is certainly the right course of action. As they prayed and sought godly wisdom, however, they had the opportunity to make various choices and still have confidence they were in God's will. Many responses would have been godly.

Free from Ishmael

One other illustration may help us understand the freedom we have in God's will. Josh and Claire are friends at church. While pursuing an adoption from Bulgaria, a situation presented itself for them to provide a home for some children domestically. These children were seemingly in need of an immediate home, and Josh and Claire were not sure what to do. Should they abandon their current plans? What if they chose the wrong child—the Ishmael?

After carefully assessing their capabilities, considering the commitments they had already made to their agency, and spending time in prayer, Josh and Claire decided to continue to pursue their Bulgarian adoption. As they did so, they remained open to God changing their circumstances. God raised up another family to care for the other children, as our church was confident he would do.

Praise God that he guides us through Scripture and his Spirit, and sovereignly directs our every step. May you and I pursue his revealed will with renewed vigor and have confidence in his leading as we make decisions with humility.

SMALL GROUP DISCUSSION GUIDE

FELLOWSHIP AND PRAYER

STARTER QUESTIONS
1. What is a decision you are struggling with as you think about caring for the fatherless?
2. What are some ways you have heard people express their understanding of God's will?

SCRIPTURE TO CONSIDER
1. Read Isaiah 46:1–11. What does this tell you about God's will?
2. Look through the following passages and identify whether each is referring to God's will of decree or his will of desire:

   • Mark 3:35

   • John 1:13

   • Romans 15:32

   • Ephesians 1:1

   • Ephesians 6:5–7

   • Colossians 4:12

   • Hebrews 10:36

   • 1 John 2:17

   • Revelation 4:11

REVIEWING PRINCIPLES FROM THE CHAPTER
1. What is meant by God's decreed will? How does understanding that aspect of God's will impact our life? How should we view the plans we make for our life?
2. What is meant by God's declared will? What are some clear instructions that God has given that you struggle to obey? Can you think of ways your obedience might help you with decisions you need to make?
3. What are some of the mistakes people make as they search for God to direct specific decisions they must make? What are some unbiblical ways that people search for guidance?
4. What are some of the things we can be confident of as we speak of God's will?

APPLICATION QUESTIONS

1. What are some of the big decisions you need to make in your life regarding orphan care ministry? List the top five to ten decisions that need to be made.

2. Look at the suggestions in this chapter given in the section "God's Will and the Orphan." How can they be applied to the decisions you listed?

9 The Orphan *and the* Church

There might not be an orphan ministry at our church today if we had not first been introduced to Kristina.

Before age five, Kristina had lived with her mother and been exposed to some things to which no one, especially a young child, should be exposed. Her mother's love for drugs exceeded her love for her own children, and Kristina was taken from her mother's care and placed in the care of her father.

Things did not fare well for her at her father's either. Her father was often gone and would work late hours. When he was home, he drank. A lot. And when her father drank, he would sometimes become physically abusive. In the eighth grade, the Department of Children and Family Services removed Kristina from her home and placed her in the foster system.

She was placed in the home of one of our members and that is how she became connected with our church. Seeing the Lord work in her life was an eye-opening experience for me. Her life was a dramatic testimony to the things the Lord could accomplish in the lives of children through the faithfulness of his saints.

At the church she became a part of a new family. She lived with her foster family for only six months, "but those were the most important six months of my life," she says.

Eventually, Kristina was placed back in the care of her father, but that was not the end of her involvement with the church. Following her graduation from high school, she began attending the church plant I pastor. As she became plugged into the life of the church, she was welcomed in by people who had never known her.

When she gave her testimony at her baptism, Kristina recalled the love her foster family had shown her and how it had affected her:

> I was accepted into their family as soon as I stepped out of the car to meet them for the first time. I instantly fell in love with this family. They were now MY family. They showed me what it was

147

like to love people and be loved. They treated me just like I was their own daughter. But most importantly, they showed me the way to Jesus Christ. On November 4, 2004, I prayed for Jesus to come into my heart, asking him to be the Lord and savior of my life. I began attending Bethany Baptist Church.

After her baptismal testimony, a family was so moved by her story that they invited her to participate in the life of their family. She became an integral part of their family, and even lived with them for awhile. The church was able to offer Kristina exactly what she needed: a family.

The Concept of Community

The church is tailor-made for the child who needs a family. We fail to understand the significance of that because the concept of community is a hard one for our culture to grasp. Even for those of us who are part of the church and are called by God to participate in a community, the nature of that fellowship can be somewhat hazy. Over the past several decades in North America, there has been a seismic shift in our perception concerning what a relationship is and how it functions. We have entered the age of the "technological tribe" or the "Facebook fellowship."

Relationships in the technological tribe are extensive and exciting. You know a large number of people who are all over the globe. With a few clicks of the mouse you can find out how your best friend from sixth grade who now lives in Taiwan is doing. Even though you are driving in a car in the Midwest, your voice can be put on a speaker phone in New York. If you want to contact me, you can call me at home, work, or at the grocery store. You can e-mail me or text me. And we are so addicted to this feeling of connection that it is inevitable that, even if you initially fail to reach me all those locations, it will not be long before I find out that you are trying to reach me.

But in the technological tribe, there are problems as well. We are simultaneously both better connected and more alone than ever. While I may know what a person in another continent had for breakfast, I do not know the name of my next-door neighbor. I am sitting in a coffee shop texting a friend from church but will never speak to the person who is seated at the next table. Shane Hipps describes this illusory community as a "virtual community" that is "infinitely more virtual than it is communal. It's a bit like cotton candy: It goes down easy and satiates our immediate hunger, but it doesn't provide much in the way of sustainable nutrition. Not

only that, but our appetite is spoiled. We no longer feel the need to participate in authentic community. Authentic community involves high degrees
of intimacy, permanence, and proximity. While relative intimacy can be
gained in virtual settings, the experiences of permanence and proximity
have all but vanished."[1]

Our tribal relationships can be shallow and fragile. There is physical
space that separates us, and so you only know as much about me as I choose
to reveal. When you get too close, I can let our friendship wither by not
answering your e-mails or avoiding your calls when your name pops up on
my cell phone.

The social networking site Facebook is the perfect tool for the technological tribe. I know you through Twitter-length bursts. Instead of inter-
acting with you over a meal, I can digitally poke you. I may not know that
you and your spouse spent all night screaming at one another about the
overdue bills, but thanks to social networking, I know that you are "having
sloppy joes tonight."

Do not misunderstand me. The tools of the technological tribe—
like Twitter and Facebook—can be incredibly useful as a supplement to
genuine community. I have been amazed how Christians have encouraged
and strengthened one another through the use of blogs and social networking sites. We should not, however, confuse real, deep, vibrant community with what passes for a friendship in the age of the technological
tribe.

If the church is to care for orphans in the way that God calls her to,
it is vital that she understand the concepts of family and community. This
chapter will focus on a few core theological truths regarding the nature of
the church that reveal why and how it must care for the fatherless.

Christ Created a Family

Alexander Strauch, in his seminal book on eldership, argues that we
have often misunderstood the biblical role of an elder because we have
failed to grasp that the church is a family. "Of the different New Testament
terms used to describe the nature of the church—the body, the bride,
the temple, the flock—the most frequently used is the family, particularly
the fraternal aspect of the family, *brethren*."[2] The usage is not accidental,
continues Strauch: "The reason behind this preference for the familial

---

1. Hipps, *Flickering Pixels*, 114.
2. Strauch, *Biblical Eldership*, 109.

aspect of the church is that only the most intimate of human relationships could express the love, closeness, privileges, and relationships that exist between God and man, and man and man, as a result of Christ's incarnation and death. The local Christian church, then, is to be a close-knit family of brothers and sisters."[3]

Family Versus Corporation

God calls the church to exhibit the characteristics of a family. Unfortunately, churches both large and small are looking instead to the corporate world for a model on how to function. Pastors become CEOs and elders and deacons become members of a board.

Consider just a few contrasts between a family and a corporation:

* A corporation sacrifices an individual for the common good.
  A family sacrifices for the good of the individual.
* Membership in a corporation is voluntary and temporary.
  Membership in a family is mandatory and permanent.
* Relationships in a corporation are based upon mutual benefit.
  Relationships within a family are based upon sacrificial love.
* The leader of a corporation is a CEO.
  The leader of a family is a shepherd.

When church leadership takes on the characteristics of a corporate board, what is left for the congregation to become but consumers? David Wells describes one way the church's corporate model has affected the congregation:

The evangelical church, or at least a good slice of it, is nervous, twitchy, and touchy about consumer desire, ready to change in a nanosecond at the slightest hint that tastes and interests have changed. Why? Because consumer appetite reigns. And consumer appetite and consumer rights go hand in hand. These rights and appetites are very much alive in what used to be called the pew. Those who attend churches are not like any other customers you might meet in the mall. Displease them in any way and they will take their business elsewhere. That is the fear that lurks in many a church leader's soul because they know that is how the market-place works.[4]

3. Ibid, 110.
4. Wells, *The Courage to Be Protestant*, 36.

Christ did not create a corporation when he created his church. In Ephesians 2:14–18, Paul describes the creation of the church. As we examine this text it becomes clear that the church is a family—God's family—and this helps us begin to understand what the church has to offer the fatherless.

Christ Destroyed the Division (vv. 14–15a)

A wall both physically and symbolically separates people. In "The Mending Wall," Robert Frost's narrator reluctantly repairs the wall between him and his neighbor, observing that "before I built a wall I'd ask to know what I was walling in or walling out."

Christ destroyed those things that divide people. Paul writes: "For he himself is our peace, who has made us both one and has broken down in his flesh the dividing wall of hostility by abolishing the law of commandments expressed in ordinances" (Eph. 2:14–15a). Be it racism or class or culture or bitterness, Christ destroys the barrier and creates peace. In fact, Paul tells us, Christ is our peace (v. 14), he makes peace (v. 15) and proclaims peace (v. 17). This peace cannot be found elsewhere.

The peace that he brings is not just an absence of hostility between groups that hate one another, but rather a true creation of God's *shalom*, or peace. When a mom separates her children who are fighting into different rooms, she has accomplished a cessation of active warfare, but she has not created biblical peace and harmony.

The orphan has known tragedy, not peace. The most intimate relationship in that child's world has been shattered. The loss that is experienced by an orphan is difficult to comprehend. Even the child may never be able to express in words exactly how that loss affects him. He has experienced a separation in his physical life that is illustrative of the separation that we all have in our spiritual lives. Each of us has experienced the tragedy of separation from one another and separation from God the Father.

How radical, then, is this peace that Christ creates. He "has made us both one and has broken down in his flesh the dividing wall of hostility" (v. 14). When different groups come together in Christ, there is true integration and a family bond that goes even deeper than the relationships we have within our biological family. One new man is created in place of the two. This peace was made possible because of Christ's death on the cross. The barriers to fellowship with God are removed. We come into relationship with him and with one another through faith in his Son.

In my study, I have a piece of concrete with some graffiti on it. It is a piece of the Berlin Wall that my aunt gave me and is one of my most prized possessions. The Berlin Wall was constructed in 1961 by the communists to separate the East from the West. Guards on the east side were ordered to use lethal force on anyone trying to breach the wall. Over the next few decades, some 200 people would lose their lives trying to cross into the West. Many would be successful. Some would jump from apartment buildings. Some would float over in hot air balloons. In the early days, one person drove a sports car through a hastily constructed barrier.

In the fall of 1989, communist regimes began to topple. East Germans began to escape into the West through other countries. West Berliners gathered at the wall and at first chanted, "We want in." Then, the chant slowly began to change. "We're staying here," they proclaimed, boldly demanding that the East Germans be allowed to experience the freedom the West had to offer.

On November 9, 1989, an official from East Germany held a press conference and, confused by some communication he had received, stated that travel between the East and West was permissible effective immediately. Tens of thousands of East Germans flooded the streets and made their way to the walls. Guards at checkpoints were overwhelmed. "Wall woodpeckers" began to take sledgehammers to portions of the wall. If you are old enough to remember the fall of the Berlin Wall, surely some of the scenes of men and women destroying it and the throngs of people celebrating are etched into your mind. A barrier of division had come down. Families were reunited. Peace was achieved.

Christ has broken down for his church a barrier that is far more divisive than the Berlin Wall. Proclaiming the news of peace and reconciliation to the world is now the unique privilege of the church. We take the message of peace and proclaim it to all, especially those who are most desperate for it. The fatherless, those who have known tragedy, must hear about the peace that Christ has created and the barrier that has been removed so that a relationship with their heavenly Father is possible.

Christ Created the Church (vv. 15b–16)

It is important to keep in mind that when Christ destroyed the divisions separating people, he simultaneously created the church. Paul writes that Christ did so "that he might create in himself one new man in place of the two, so making peace, and might reconcile us both to God in one body through the cross, thereby killing the hostility" (Eph. 2:15b–16). The church could not exist within the framework of the Old Testament law.

Whitney and I have several pieces of furniture that have been "well-loved." Being thrifty folks, we made it through our first ten years of marriage without purchasing any new furniture, save a rocking chair. Instead, we made garage sale purchases and took the generous used furniture donations of our friends and family members, some donated unknowingly in the dark of night.

One of our garage sale purchases was a $4 coffee table. It was over-priced. It is my belief someone was throwing it away and pretended it was a garage sale item when Whitney made an inquiry about it.

The coffee table received a fresh coat of paint, but it remained an old, used coffee table. The drawers were in constant need of repair, the edges were scuffed. As a joke, we put coasters on the table. When guests put their glasses on the table, in mock horror we would quickly pick them up and put them on a coaster. After ten years of marriage, we finally purchased a brand new coffee table.

The church is a new creation. It is not just a refurbished version of Israel. It is brand spanking new. It is a new creation that is marked by its unity. Christ creates one new man in place of the two. The new creation experiences fellowship with other believers that is a taste of the fellowship experienced within the Trinity. The fellowship we have is the fulfillment of the prayer Jesus prays in John 17:21, asking that we "may all be one, just as you, Father, are in me, and I in you."

What does this have to do with the orphan? Don't you see! A new family is created by Christ, and it is precisely a family that the orphan desperately needs. In fact, the unity that the spiritual family possesses gives the fatherless something even greater than a biological family.

Christ Proclaimed Our Peace (vv. 17–18)

The peace Christ provided did not stay a secret. It was proclaimed by Christ. Paul writes, "And he came and preached peace to you who were far off and peace to those who were near. For through him we both have access in one Spirit to the Father" (Eph. 2:17–18).

This wonderful reality is now proclaimed by the believer to all who have the opportunity to hear. Peace with God is available, through faith alone in Christ alone. It provides not just the cessation of hostilities but the intimacy of relationship through the Spirit to God the Father—Father!

Many of us owe the church so much. It is the church through which God proclaimed his gospel, the message of his son Jesus Christ. The church proclaimed the gospel to my parents. The church discipled my parents. The church provided my parents with accountability and models for a godly home. The church dedicated me in my infancy. The church loved me as a child. The church taught me about my Savior. The church taught me the Scriptures. The church proclaimed the gospel to me. The church loved me. The church rejoiced in my salvation. The church baptized me. The church provided for my training in ministry. The church now provides for my family. The church is my family, and it is Christ's church that I love and I will defend

I desperately want the orphan to know the church and experience the family relationships she offers. I want to give the orphan not only food and shelter but a spiritual home. I want the gospel to penetrate the orphan's heart in such a way that he learns about the peace of God that is found only in Christ. It is only the church that can provide the orphan with true community and family.

Christ Gave Gifts to His Church

The church is also in a unique position to care for orphans because of the gifts Christ has given to his body. In fact, it is *only* the church that possesses the spiritual gifts necessary to meet all the needs of the orphan.

Have you ever thought about who the most important person in your church is? I try in vain to convince the people in my church that it is the senior pastor, but they are far too discerning. As the primary teaching pastor, I have the opportunity to talk for forty minutes (or so) without interruption (unless you count crying babies and repentant sinners). No one else in the church has that privilege. But as important as that time is, it is just a fraction of the ministry that our church is doing. God creates and maintains tremendous ministries in his church without my involvement.

The question of who is the most important person in the church is a ridiculous question, for no member could function without the others or without the equipping work of the Spirit. Each person in our church is necessary for the body to function effectively.

Spiritual Gifts Are Gifts of Grace

Each member of the body has been given a spiritual gift and that is one reason orphan care ministry must be supported by the church as a whole and not done by the individual alone.

Contrary to what many think about the burdensome nature of ministry, God did not give spiritual gifts to the church as a punishment. The believer should not view ministry like a child views his chores. God calls the believer to utilize his or her gifts for the benefit of the body. This command is not to bring gloom and weariness to the heart but joy!

Christ Gives Diverse Gifts

The gifts that have been given to believers are incredibly diverse. Many spiritual gift quizzes have been designed in order to help people "find" their spiritual gifts. As I look at Scriptures describing spiritual gifts, however, it seems more accurate to see these manifestations of grace as being so diverse that the biblical writers are only able to describe them using broad, general categories. There are several texts that give us a perspective of the diversity of the gifts that the church possesses. In Romans 12, Paul refers to "gifts that differ." The purpose is to "use them: if prophecy, in proportion to our faith; if service, in our serving; the one who teaches, in his teaching; the one who exhorts, in his exhortation; the one who contributes, in generosity; the one who leads, with zeal; the one who does acts of mercy, with cheerfulness" (vv. 6–8). In 1 Corinthians 12:7–10, he will describe how each person has been given a "manifestation of the Spirit" and then give various examples.

In Ephesians 4:13–16, Paul paints a thrilling picture of a body operating in harmony as it grows together. It is a picture that can only be true of the local church. Let me state that more personally: You have a gift that no one else in your church has. The church cannot be what it was meant to be without you exercising that gift. The church cannot do all the ministries she was called to do without you. And you cannot do the ministries you have been called to do without her support and nurture.

Why You and the Parachurch Cannot Care Adequately for the Orphan

The call to care for orphans is a collective call. It cannot be met by an individual alone but requires the effort of the entire church.

Jason and Carolyn are a couple whose lives were touched by the local church. They had struggled with infertility and, over the years, considered adoption as a possibility to grow their family.

"We had talked about adoption," says Carolyn, "but we were stalled out on getting anywhere. Then, one day we saw in the bulletin that an adoption ministry was beginning. At that point, it seemed as though the adoption ministry was starting up just for us."

They began to attend the Bible study and were extremely encouraged. The Bible study presented an opportunity for them to discuss biblical truths with other believers. Every week, they were being exposed to God's truth regarding orphans and later debriefing as a couple. "The Bible study was excellent. It opened up communication between us. It was tremendous and because of that Bible study, over those weeks, God really moved in our hearts to help us to see that the two of us were to adopt a sibling group," says Carolyn.

There was more to the involvement of the local church. Through our church's orphan ministry Jason and Carolyn spent time with others who had been through the adoption process to help them through the next steps and encourage them. "The Open Hearts, Open Homes ministry offered encouragement, guidance in our process," says Carolyn. "I can't imagine we would have ever gone forward in our adoption without the help of the ministry," contends Jason. "Our adoption would not have happened without the adoption ministry coming alongside of us and giving us encouragement."

The help of the local church was not limited to those in the church who were already passionate about orphan care. Jason and Carolyn's Sunday school class cared for them and assisted them in their preparations. Those who were skilled workers came out and made modifications to their home. The class received weekly updates on where they were in their process. A blog was set up and posted on. Many people in the church contributed financially to their adoption expenses. A loan they had planned on taking out was rendered unnecessary as the body of Christ came together.

Jason and Carolyn happened to be gone to pick up their children when our church celebrated Orphan Sunday. I showed pictures of their time in Colombia from the pulpit. When they came home, an entire church enveloped the children (when the time was appropriate, of course).

"We would never have been bold enough to go down this path without our church," Jason later said. God brought Jason and Carolyn's children home through the collaborative efforts of the church. The local church taught on the importance of caring for orphans. Those with gifts of giving helped financially. Those with gifts of service worked on their home. Everyone came together to bring these three precious children home.

We must not understate the role that the parachurch played in bringing their children home. Lifesong for Orphans, for example, handled the financial aspects of the adoption in ways that the church could not. It also provided invaluable insight regarding other aspects of the adoption process.

Yet, God did not promise to strengthen and equip the parachurch organization. The local church can meet the needs of orphans in a way that no other institution on earth can because of the spiritual gifts with which God has equipped her.

Do not be discouraged if your church does not immediately grasp the joy of ministering to children. It was the presence of a foster child in our church that opened my eyes to the truths of Scripture. It was the presence of Jason and Carolyn that transformed the lives of many in a Sunday school class. As the body begins to see how God operates in its midst, the Spirit will do the equipping work that only he can do.

SMALL GROUP DISCUSSION GUIDE

FELLOWSHIP AND PRAYER

STARTER QUESTIONS

1. Do you believe that the church understands "community"? Why or why not?
2. How were you first made aware of the need to care for the fatherless?

SCRIPTURE TO CONSIDER

1. Read Ephesians 2:11–22 and list the characteristics of the unity Christ has brought about.
2. Read through 1 Corinthians 12:4–7. What does it mean that there are a variety of gifts? Why are gifts given? What does verse 11 teach us about the giving of gifts?
3. See Application Question #1 for additional verses to consider.

REVIEWING PRINCIPLES FROM THE CHAPTER

1. In what ways is the church "tailor made" for the orphan?
2. What are some of the truths that are important to keep in mind as we consider that Christ has created a family? How does that impact our care for orphans?
3. Why has God given spiritual gifts to the church? How do the spiritual gifts uniquely equip the church to care for the orphan?

APPLICATION QUESTIONS

1. Think through the various spiritual gifts that are given to the church (Rom. 12:6–8, 1 Cor. 12:7–10, 28). How might each of these gifts be necessary for a healthy orphan ministry?
2. As you think through what Christ has done to create a community, what are the implications for those of us who claim we cannot have unity with some Christians?
3. What are some ways that your church could be exposed to the joy of orphan ministry?

10 Church Leadership *and an* Orphan Ministry

Speaking as a senior pastor, let me just say something in a spirit of love to those of you who are passionate about orphans.

You people scare me.

Your passion, though commendable, is off-putting. You have garage sales to raise funds for orphans. You blog obsessively. You pray for and cry over other people's adopted children whom you have never met. You consider other orphan advocates as friends even if your relationship is only virtual. You take out second mortgages on your homes. You eat beans to save money. You drive an old vehicle because you are preparing to spend tens of thousands of dollars to care for some kid you have never met.

Who does that sort of stuff? That's right. *Scary* people. And by scary, I mean people whose commitment level frightens the rest of us because of its implications for our lives.

So, speaking as a senior pastor, let me say it again: You scare me. You scare me individually and *really* scare me as a herd.

The good news is that I am also one of you. I have been assimilated. And, because of my dual role as Orphan Dad and Senior Pastor, I am bilingual—I can be misunderstood in two languages simultaneously: Pastor-speak and Orphan-speak. I hope that throughout the book I have been speaking bilingually, but it is especially important that I do so here.

In addition to all your other fanatical tendencies, you also desire your church to be a refuge for orphans. You read the previous chapter regarding the importance of the church in the life of the orphan and felt a sense of longing and excitement. And so you are planning to contact your church leaders and want to know the best way to proceed. Or you have already met with them and were disappointed that they did not respond with the vigor you expected.

This chapter is meant to be a resource for you as you approach your church leaders. God has entrusted your soul to this group of people. And you need to think through—biblically—how to understand, communicate with, and respond to them. Any success our church has had in caring for orphans is due in large part to the faithfulness of the men in leadership at our church.[1]

Before we continue, I should clarify something pertinent to this chapter's discussion. I am assuming you are in a church that understands and proclaims the gospel, preaches God's Word, and has leaders who are committed to shepherding Christ's church. If you are not in such a church, you need to do everything you can to get in one. I do not mean that you must be in a church that always obeys God perfectly, or that you must be in a church that agrees with you on every point of doctrine. I mean that you should attend a church that is faithful to the gospel message and God's Word.[2]

Understanding Spiritual Shepherds

Our first task is to consider what a church leader is and what he is to do. To each local church, Christ has given men who are entrusted with the task of shepherding, or leading, that church.

What's in a Name?

There are several words that the New Testament writers employ to refer to the leaders of the church. Though some churches make distinctions between these terms and treat them as different offices, I believe Scripture uses terms like "pastor," "elder," and "overseer" interchangeably to refer to the same office.[3] Our church is led by a group of men we refer to as "elders." As the senior pastor, I serve as a paid elder but have equal authority and responsibility with the other shepherds of our church. You do not need to agree with my understanding of church governance, however, to apply the biblical principles in this chapter. The main truth to be gleaned from this discussion is that Christ has appointed men to shepherd his church.

Responsibilities of the Shepherds of a Church

The shepherds in your church have been given an awesome stewardship. They are leaders, as demonstrated by the titles "overseer" and "elder."

---

1. For a discussion and defense of male leadership in the church, see some of the material produced by the Council for Biblical Manhood and Womanhood (www.cbmw.org). See, e.g., Piper and Grudem, "What Does the Bible Say About Leadership in the Church?"
2. See Mark Dever, *Nine Marks of a Healthy Church* (Wheaton: Crossway, 2004).
3. E.g., Acts 20:17, 28 and 1 Peter 5:1–2a.

The type of leadership they are to exercise, however, is not a harsh leadership, but rather a shepherding or "pastoral" leadership that is characterized by gentleness (see 1 Tim. 5:17; 1 Peter 5:2–5).

There are many components to this task of shepherding the flock. One of the primary responsibilities is to teach. The teaching ministry is so important that in Acts 6 the leaders in the church turn over the responsibilities of caring for widows to the deacons, telling the congregation, "we will devote ourselves to prayer and to the ministry of the word" (v. 4).

Their teaching also helps them fulfill their responsibility to protect the flock from doctrines and beliefs that would undermine the health of the church. Notice Paul's warning to the elders from Ephesus:

> Pay careful attention to yourselves and to all the flock, in which the Holy Spirit has made you overseers, to care for the church of God, which he obtained with his own blood. I know that after my departure fierce wolves will come in among you, not sparing the flock; and from among your own selves will arise men speaking twisted things, to draw away the disciples after them. Therefore be alert, remembering that for three years I did not cease night or day to admonish everyone with tears. (Acts 20:28–31)

The elders protect the flock by both teaching right doctrine and refuting wrong doctrine. This is why Titus is told that an elder must "hold firm to the trustworthy word as taught, so that he may be able to give instruction in sound doctrine and also to rebuke those who contradict it" (1:9).

There are also administrative aspects of the elders' responsibilities. "So the disciples determined, everyone according to his ability, to send relief to the brothers living in Judea. And they did so, sending it to the elders by the hand of Barnabas and Saul" (Acts 11:29–30). The elders were in charge of the collection and distribution of funds within the church.

Paul refers to pastors as a gift given by God to the church. The purpose of the gift of spiritual shepherds is to equip the body to use their spiritual gifts: "And he gave the apostles, the prophets, the evangelists, the shepherds [pastors] and teachers, to equip the saints for the work of ministry, for building up the body of Christ …" (Eph. 4:11).

Observe a profound difference between what this text says about the role of the pastor and the way the church often views the role of a pastor. Ephesians tells us pastors do not do all the ministry in a church. They train others to do the work of ministry. In other words, it is not the task of the pastor to care for the orphans. It is not the responsibility of the pastor to discern exactly how all the administrative details will be handled. It is the job of the pastor to equip others through teaching and prayer so that they can perform the tasks God has prepared for them to do.

I have no ministry horror stories. I love my job and I do not believe I am unduly burdened. I have no complaints about my work load. The staff and the lay people I serve with are diligent laborers and are gracious to me. Even so, the job of a pastor is incredibly demanding. Don't get me wrong. Even with its stresses it is a joyous labor. And I'm sure other jobs are difficult as well. I just want you to see the difficulties inherent in your pastor's job. It never ends. When the pastor is on vacation, he is just one emergency or need away from being back on call. And his mind is still back with the flock. There is no vacation from praying for the people in the church.

One of the (many) reasons I am not very much fun at parties is that I am always thinking about some aspect of ministry. The shepherding responsibilities I have are always with me. The church is one of the last thoughts I have when I go to sleep and one of the first thoughts I have when I wake up in the morning.

No matter how hard your pastor works, no matter how many hours he puts in during the week, the time is not sufficient for the needs. Sunday morning comes around every week, and no matter what else has happened during that week, people will file into the room and expect to hear from God's word.

I, for one, never feel as though the people have gotten everything they deserve from me. At the end of the week, I have not visited everyone I wanted to visit. I have not studied the way I wanted to study. I have not done the training I desired to do. I have not cared for all the needs that I know exist in the flock. All shepherds who love their flock feel this burden.

Responsibilities of the Flock

Let's pretend your pastor is sitting in his study on a Tuesday afternoon, immersed in returning phone calls, answering e-mail, and looking at an ever-expanding to-do list. He scans the list:

Return chairman's phone call
Assess evangelism ministry
Visit hospital
Begin calling discipleship group leaders
Find nursery workers for Sunday morning
Write article for newsletter
Find replacement Sunday school teacher
Appoint missions committee members . . .

As he looks through the list, he realizes there is no way that on his own strength he will ever be able to meet even the most basic needs of the church.

At this point, you walk into his study. You mention that you were "in the area" and thought you would stop by (it's not like he has a real job!). During your unscheduled visit, you lay out the biblical case for orphan care. You are passionate. You are committed. You mention that you are confident that he will begin to get the vision for this ministry and put the important pieces in place.

He is noncommittal. He does not say "no," but he does not seem to be taking notes. The glazed look on his face does not fill you with confidence. On the Sunday following your meeting, you are extremely disappointed that he does not mention orphan care from the pulpit. In the following months, you are shocked that nothing seems to have come from your meeting. Does he not know there is a *biblical mandate to care for the orphan*?

The truth of the matter is that he probably does know that. In fact, it is one more item on that ever-increasing list of things he knows the church should be doing that it is not. He wishes the church was doing better in evangelism, in youth ministry, in worship, and, truth be told, he's pretty sure his preaching is getting worse rather than better. Your pastor is so overwhelmed with his other duties that he has no time to even think about beginning a new ministry.

It is important, therefore, for those who are part of the flock to understand *their responsibilities to their spiritual shepherds.* One of the best summaries of the responsibility you have to your spiritual leaders is found in Hebrews 13:

> Remember your leaders, those who spoke to you the word of God. Consider the outcome of their way of life, and imitate their faith. Jesus Christ is the same yesterday and today and forever. Do not be led away by diverse and strange teachings, for it is good for the heart to be strengthened by grace, not by foods, which have not benefited those devoted to them.... Obey your leaders and submit to them, for they are keeping watch over your souls, as those who will have to give an account. Let them do this with joy and not with groaning, for that would be of no advantage to you. (vv. 7–9, 17)

It is not just the leaders who have a difficult job. Those who are part of the church must be careful to make sure that they are submitting to those who are in a position of spiritual authority over them. Do those who are your spiritual leaders describe their relationship with you as one of joy or hardship?

The word *submission* means to willingly place oneself underneath the authority of another. Submission to leaders in any context is difficult and it is a concept with which many believers struggle. Bruce Ware offers this profound thought regarding submission as he discusses the relationship between God the Father and God the Son and its application to our lives:

> How remarkable that within the Godhead, not only is authority eternally exercised, but submission marks the relationship of the Son to the Father from eternity past to eternity future. How astonishing to realize that it is just as Godlike to submit gladly and joyfully to rightful authority as it is Godlike to exercise legitimate, rightful authority. Our tendency is to think of God as the one who has absolute authority, and of course this is true. But less known and little understood is the alternate truth that in God eternal submission to authority is also exercised. All of us, in one way or another, are in positions of submission. Certainly, wives to their husbands, children to their parents, congregations to their elders, employees to their employers, and citizens to their governments—all of us live in submission to one or more authority. Can we learn from Jesus what it means to be "Godlike" in submitting? Rather than despising authority, or even rather than yielding to authority with a grumbling and begrudging spirit, we learn from Jesus just what true submission looks like. May God grant us eyes to see the beauty of rightful authority and rightful submission, and may we seek to model our lives, by God's grace, more after the way Jesus lives always and only to please the Father.[4]

The submission God calls us to, Ware observes, has already been modeled perfectly by Christ. If God is willing to submit himself, how much more should we humbly submit to those in leadership? Your other responsibilities to leaders include praying for them, being accountable to their leadership (Heb. 13:17; 1 Peter 5:5), and, as much as possible, making it a joy for them to be in ministry (Heb. 13:17).

It is not difficult to notice how spiritual shepherds are failing in their ministry to us. It hurts when they forget our names or fail to notice when we go through difficult times. Once, there was a man in our church whose mother passed away. To our shame, no one on the staff contacted him. I can

---

4. Ware, *Father, Son, and Holy Spirit*, 98–99.

still remember reading the letter he wrote to the leaders, understandably expressing pain that no one from the church had even called him to see how he was doing. Our lapse there was serious and inexcusable. We had to ask for his forgiveness.

Shepherds are going to fail you in noticeable ways. The ways in which we fail our spiritual shepherds may be less obvious. Are we faithfully praying for them? Are we joyfully submitting to them? God has called both shepherds and the flock to minister to one another.

Approaching Church Leaders About an Orphan Ministry

Based on the responsibilities shepherds have, they bear the primary responsibility for overseeing the development and implementation of an orphan ministry. It may be that your spiritual leaders have never thought about the possibility of beginning an orphan ministry. Or they may have considered it but were unsure as to how to proceed.

I mentioned earlier that one of the reasons our orphan ministry has done well is because our church was blessed with great spiritual shepherds. Just as important to any success God has granted us has been lay leaders in the church who took it upon themselves to do the work of the ministry. Without their tireless efforts and labor, our ministry would have floundered.

Unbiblical Ways to Influence Church Leaders

At the orphanage where she spent the first year and a half of her life, Ellie learned something interesting. When there are fifty to seventy kids who want something, the one who complains the loudest often gets her way. When we brought her home, her whining gave a whole new spin on the phrase "the cry of the orphan." She soon found that what had been successful in the orphanage was not effective with her new mom and dad.

There are some unbiblical ways you can get what you want in a family and in a church. Manipulation is unbiblical but often effective. If you are in a church and the leaders of the church are not moving forward to care for orphans, or moving forward in a different direction or more slowly than you would like, I have some (terrible) suggestions on how you could try to force the leaders in your church to give you what you want.

Try grumbling. The smaller your church, the more effective grumbling can be. If the leaders do not do what you desire, complain. Any time you have a conversation with your leaders, bring up the orphan ministry. Refuse to be involved in any other ministry. Withhold tithing to the church and give it to orphan ministries, justifying your actions by thinking about how your church is failing to do what God wants them to do. At some point, your complaints will make their way to the leaders. Negative comments are far more powerful than positive comments and have a corrosive effect on the morale of leaders. Even if they disagree with your opinion, there is a possibility that grumbling against the leaders will wear them down to the point that they will go along with what you want them to do.

Seriously now, the only problem with this form of influence is that it is completely and thoroughly unbiblical. Your responsibility to the leaders is to make shepherding you a joy. Additionally, Philippians 2:14 instructs us that all things should be done without grumbling or complaining. When the people of Israel grumbled against their leaders, it was revealed to them that they were grumbling against the Lord (Num. 16:11).

Do not grumble against the leaders God has placed over you. I trust it is your desire to maintain a godly and encouraging attitude toward the leadership of your church. Of course, this does not mean it is wrong to confront the leaders of a church when necessary. It does mean that we must always be careful to avoid an attitude of complaining or grumbling in our dealings with our spiritual shepherds.

Don't back down! Another way to influence your church leaders is to stubbornly resist their leadership. Stand your ground! Don't let anyone push you around! Sometimes church conflicts are won by those who refuse to flinch.

Again, the problem with this method is that it is unbiblical. Persistence can be a good thing, but persistence borne of an unsubmissive spirit is sinful. Peter exhorts the younger men in the church with an instruction that is applicable to all: "Likewise, you who are younger, be subject to the elders. Clothe yourselves, all of you, with humility toward one another, for 'God opposes the proud but gives grace to the humble'" (1 Peter 5:5; cf. Heb. 13:17).

An unsubmissive spirit manifests itself in very visible ways. It fails to receive instruction or go along with a decision that has been reached. It is quick to point out negative consequences of decisions it does not agree with. It quickly engages in conflict and seeks its own way.

When we approach our leaders, our desire should be obedience to God in the area of submission. When the leaders urges caution or even takes us in a direction different from the one we would wish to go, our heart's attitude should be one of willing submission to the leading of the Spirit.

Spread gossip and dissension. There is strength in numbers. Your voice alone may not be powerful enough to enact true change within your church. If you want to increase your ability to influence the leadership, get other folks involved in the act. Ask your Sunday school class to "pray for the leaders because they apparently lack a love for children."

To truly be effective at gossip, go beyond the walls of the church. Mention to others how poor of a job your church is doing in the area of orphan care. Complain to relatives and friends how disappointed you are with your church. If you are effective at gossip, at some point there may be such an outcry against the leaders that you can stand back and let others do the dirty work. Or, the climate may be so poisoned that no ministry is able to be done well.

Seriously now, this approach suffers once again from the minor problem of being utterly sinful. Remember that the church is a family. When you attack the church you are attacking Christ's family—which presumably includes you!

Early on in our marriage, Whitney and I agreed that any conflicts we had would be discussed only between the two of us or, if ever necessary, with a party who had the ability to help bring about resolution to our disagreement. We did this because we each wanted the strongest relational bond in our lives to be the one between us. I did not want my discussion of a conflict or disagreement to cause another person to "take my side" against my wife (or, worse yet, my wife's side against me). I wanted it to be clear to everyone: to side against my wife is to side against me as well. Whitney and I are partners and we wanted everyone in our lives to know that.

What is true in a marriage should be true in a church. Paul writes in 2 Corinthians 12:20, " For I fear that perhaps when I come I may find you not as I wish, and that you may find me not as you wish—that perhaps there may be quarreling, jealousy, anger, hostility, slander, gossip, conceit, and disorder." We are responsible to preserve the unity of the church.

We have seen in Ephesians 2 that Christ has brought the church together. Ephesians 4 continues the theme of unity as Paul urges the church to "walk in a manner worthy of the calling to which you have been called, with all humility and gentleness, with patience, bearing with one another in love, eager to maintain the unity of the Spirit in the bond of peace. There is one body and one Spirit—just as you were called to the one hope that belongs to your call—one Lord, one faith, one baptism, one God and Father of all, who is over all and through all and in all" (vv. 1–6). The responsibility of the believer is to eagerly maintain the unity that Christ has created and further the bond of peace. Gossip and dissension clearly cut at the heart of the spiritual unity of the church.

It has been my experience that most individuals and couples who are struggling to get an orphan care ministry started at their church desire to be obedient in this area. They wonder how best to strongly encourage the leadership while at the same time be in submission to them. They try to resist the urge to storm the pulpit and scream "Orphan care ministry or church split!" The tension between passion for the ministry and submission to leaders can often be difficult to resolve.

Biblical Ways to Influence Church Leaders

Fortunately, God provided us with biblical ways to influence our church leaders. We need not resort to manipulative strategies when our trust is in the Lord.

Prayer. One way that God calls us to influence those to whom we are in submission is through prayer. Paul instructs Timothy, "First of all, then, I urge that supplications, prayers, intercessions, and thanksgivings be made for all people, for kings and all who are in high positions, that we may lead a peaceful and quiet life, godly and dignified in every way" (1 Tim. 2:1–2). Paul understands that prayer can influence the lives of those in leadership. He asks for prayer for himself and others because he believes in its effectiveness (2 Cor. 1:11).

As you think through how to begin an orphan ministry at your church, pray that God would work in the hearts of your leaders. This is crucial. Do not merely pray, "God, please help my leaders." Instead, search God's Word and find out what it teaches regarding prayer and then pray those prayers. Prayer is not to be a tool for manipulating the leaders to do your will. Your prayers for them are to influence them to be the leaders God has called them to be.

Testimonies. Testimonies are another biblical way of influencing church leaders. In Acts 11, Jewish believers are skeptical when they hear about Peter's ministry to the Gentiles: "So when Peter went up to Jerusalem, the circumcision party criticized him, saying, 'You went to uncircumcised men and ate with them'" (v. 2–3). Peter responds with a testimony of God's work among the Gentiles, explaining in detail the conversion of Cornelius. The response of those who had previously been critical is to fall silent, then they "glorified God, saying, 'Then to the Gentiles also God has granted repentance that leads to life'" (v. 18).

Later in Acts, Paul approaches the leaders of the church in Jerusalem and is accompanied by Gentile converts. He understands the tension that has existed within the Jerusalem church, and so he continues to influence the leaders by having them hear stories of God's grace. Luke tells us that Paul "related one by one the things that God had done among the Gentiles through his ministry. And when they heard it, they glorified God" (21:19–20a).

In both these circumstances, those who are initially skeptical end up glorifying God as they hear about his work. Perhaps your leaders are skeptical that God's hand is truly in your plans for an orphan ministry. For me, seeing God at work in the lives of young people in our church was enormously influential in opening my heart to the biblical injunctions to care for the orphan.

Loving, humble admonishment. Another way to influence leaders is through biblical instruction, which may even include loving admonishment, done in a spirit of submission. An example of this influence is also found in Acts at the Jerusalem council. Here, as there is a discussion made concerning whether or not Gentile believers must become Jewish, God's authoritative word is appealed to (e.g., Acts 15:16–17). The admonishment must be stronger at some times than at others. Paul is very strong in his rebuke of Peter, telling us in Galatians that he "opposed him to his face" (2:11). If church leaders continue to sin, a biblical way to influence them is to have them removed from their office (1 Tim. 5:19–20)!

Practical Suggestions for Approaching Your Church Leaders

In addition to these general principles regarding how to influence leaders, here are some specific suggestions for approaching the church leaders about beginning an orphan ministry.

Be involved in ministry. First, be involved in existing ministries. It may sound strange to those of us who have a passion for the fatherless, but orphan care ministry is not the only ministry in the church. We should understand that and be aware of and involved in other ministries.

Your personal involvement in existing ministries at your church is important for several reasons. A lack of involvement in ministry indicates you are in disobedience to God regarding your commitment to the body. It reveals immaturity, and a growth in spiritual maturity will help prepare you to implement a ministry to orphans. Finally, it is important for you to know and appreciate the needs of the church before you begin asking for resources for a new ministry. It will demonstrate your concern not just for a pet project but for the needs of the body.

Know the leaders's vision for the church. As you hear your church leaders talk, what gets them most excited? Pay attention to the overall direction your leaders are trying to steer the church. If they are available in writing, read your church's vision statement, values, and goals. Go to church business meetings. Do all that you can to understand the heartbeat and concerns of your leaders. This will allow you to think through how the orphan ministry would support and interact with existing ministries.

It may sometimes seem that your leaders have "no vision." This is probably not true (although, if it is true, that is helpful to know as well!). I once heard a pastor spend half an hour laying out a vision for the church, and the very next words out of someone's mouth were, "But I feel like we as a church don't really have a vision for where we're headed." What this person meant was that he either didn't like the pastor's vision or wanted him to use some corporate buzzwords to lay out the vision of the church.

Strive to understand how God is working on the leaders of your church and how you can come alongside of them. Pray that God would give them the grace to faithfully lead his church. Pray too that God would protect you from a critical spirit and allow your leaders to experience joy through your faithfulness in ministry.

Do not expect leaders to do the ministry. Your expectation in beginning the orphan care ministry should not be that your pastor is going to lead the charge in recruiting and directing leaders for the ministry. There is a misconception that the senior pastor has the ability to convince people to do ministry in the church. The truth is that he is usually woefully ineffective at cajoling people into long-term ministry. In my experience, the most effective ministries in the church are those that passionate lay people have developed.

It is best to see the pastor and other leaders as resources to help direct the ministry. The healthiest churches are going to be those in which spiritual leaders provide a high level of feedback and initial direction to ministry and then give lay leaders the freedom to carry out the ministry on their own.

Approach the leaders with humility. Scripture calls us to consider the example of Christ's humility as we handle interpersonal relationships within the church, "Do nothing from rivalry or conceit, but in humility count others more significant than yourselves. Let each of you look not only to his own, but also to the interests of others. Have this mind among yourselves, which is yours in Christ Jesus" (Phil. 2:3–5).

If leaders and individuals faithfully practiced this principle, conflict in the church would be eliminated. Commit in your heart before meeting with the leadership that your desire is for God to be glorified in the ministry. Your passion cannot be for your proposal. Enter the meeting with the understanding that your plan could be the wrong plan for your church.

Approach the leaders with a well-researched plan. Before you get to the nuts and bolts of how the ministry works, first make sure you give adequate biblical support for the ministry. The point at which you present a plan and how much of a plan you present may vary from church to church. The point is not that you go into a meeting with your church leaders with a detailed proposal, but rather that you have enough of an understanding of how a ministry might look that you can help the leaders gain a vision for the ministry. The beginning of your presentation to the leaders might focus on the theology of orphan care ministry and why God is passionate for the fatherless. Second, make sure you show how orphan care ministry has worked at other churches, especially in churches of a similar size and philosophy of ministry. If possible, provide some testimonies of individuals in your church who have already been ministering to orphans. This can go a long way in helping alleviate concerns and questions. Third, the leaders should see that you have a grasp of how to begin to implement the ministry. The plan should address the goals of your orphan ministry and how you propose that those goals be met.[5] The following two chapters walk through the process of how this plays out practically.

Show the leaders the laborers. You should be cautious in recruiting people to a ministry that does not yet exist and does not yet have the approval of the church. However, it would be helpful to compile an informal list of names of people in the church who have already been involved in orphan care. Often, leaders are surprised with how many lives have been touched by this ministry. Give the leaders names of people who you think would be willing to serve in the ministry ... especially a point person!

The leaders of your church are aware of how understaffed many of its existing ministries are. The nursery is understaffed, the visitation committee is down to just Old Ned, and the children's Sunday school coordinator resigned due to intense fatigue! What an encouragement to the leadership if you were able to provide a list of people who have already expressed interest in being involved in caring for the fatherless.

Be prepared for objections. After you have begun discussions with church leadership, there are going to be numerous questions, maybe even objections. Remember that you have arrived at where you are via a journey.

---

5. See chapter 11 for a sample proposal; check out the section "Approach the Church Leaders" that discusses informal contact with church leaders.

You may have been thinking about orphan care ministry for years. In some cases, when you present the ministry to a leadership team or pastor, they have been thinking about orphan ministry for 15 or 20 minutes.

When your proposal is questioned, or even basic biblical principles are not understood, be careful how your heart responds. Do not become defensive or judgmental (with thoughts like, *if he really understood the Bible's teaching, he would not ask that question*). Instead, trust that God works in every believer's heart differently and be patient.

There are going to be lots of questions that come up. Is this a church ministry or an individual family ministry? Will this ministry distract us from our focus on the gospel? Could we support these families as they have needs instead of budgeting funds for them? Why adopt internationally when there are so many domestic children who need adopting? Why not just concentrate on missions? Aren't we already supporting missionaries who do this sort of thing? How will we get the funds for this ministry? Why is adoption so expensive? What would this do to the makeup of our church? Are our children's ministries equipped to handle children with special needs? Answer their questions with grace, and when you don't know the answer, say so.

Allow the Holy Spirit to work in the hearts of Christ's shepherds. You are not the Holy Spirit. It is not your job to convict or convince others regarding the truth of God's Word. It is your responsibility to pray that the Spirit would go before you and change hearts when needed— including your own!

Fortunately for you and me, God is a patient God. He lovingly guides us to where we need to be over a period of not just days or weeks but of years and decades. A man told me how one day God suddenly brought to mind a sermon he had heard five years ago. It dealt with an area of his life where the man was not consciously aware of his disobedience. But through the work of the Holy Spirit, suddenly the truths of the message became overwhelmingly convicting, and he worked to immediately resolve the issue where he was in disobedience to the Lord. May the Lord work in your heart and my own in such a gracious way.

Hold on loosely. It is very possible that the leaders of your church will develop a plan that is different from the one you present. Be willing to have your ideas modified substantially. Hold your plans tentatively, having a passion not for your plans but for God's glory.

Be willing to begin small. Finally, be willing to see the ministry begin with small steps. No matter the size of the church where you serve, you are dealing with a limited number of resources. The temptation can be to grow discontent as some of the elements of an orphan care ministry we would like to see implemented remain unrealized.

Last year I was e-mailing a family who wanted to use our church's material for an orphan Bible study. They were somewhat discouraged. They had attended a conference on orphan care ministry and heard story after story of how God was using various churches to do exciting things. After approaching their church leaders, they felt rebuffed. There seemed to be no excitement for the ministry. They were sad that the Lord did not begin an orphan ministry in their church. Nevertheless, the Lord did begin an orphan ministry in their church—just not in the way they were expecting. A staff member adopted. Other people from their church begin to talk with them about how to care for the fatherless. Many people responded to the pastor's call one Sunday to care for "the least of these" by trying to determine how they could become involved in orphan care ministry.

All of this happened without a coordinated leadership plan. God moved within the hearts of his saints and accomplished all that he desired in it. And God can do the same in your church.

SMALL GROUP DISCUSSION GUIDE

FELLOWSHIP AND PRAYER

Compile a list of the leaders in your church and spend some time in prayer for them. Brainstorm needs that they may have and ways God might use you to meet those needs.

STARTER QUESTIONS

1. What leaders have been influential in your Christian walk? What made them influential?
2. Have you had frustrating experiences in leading others? What did you find difficult about being a leader?

SCRIPTURE TO CONSIDER

Read Acts 20:17–38. What do you learn about the passions of a good spiritual shepherd? What do you learn about the responsibilities of a shepherd?

REVIEWING PRINCIPLES FROM THE CHAPTER

1. What are some of the responsibilities of shepherds in the church? What are some of the challenges to fulfilling those responsibilities?

2. What are some unreasonable expectations you may have had of your leaders?
3. What are some of the responsibilities you have toward your leaders? Are you a joy to shepherd?
4. What ministries are you currently serving in?

APPLICATION QUESTIONS

1. Would you be willing to try to spend some time with a spiritual shepherd in your church and his family in order to discern ways you can pray for them and assist them in ministry?
2. Would you be willing to commit to praying daily for your leadership this next month?
3. Do you have a developed plan for how your church might improve its ministry to orphans?
4. What are some possible objections someone might have to beginning an orphan care ministry? How would you answer these?

PART 3

Starting
an Orphan
Ministry in
Your Church

The temptation for many who have a passion to begin caring for orphans may be to turn to this section first. That is understandable and, truth be told, probably where I would turn to first as well. I hope that if you read this section first, you will go back and read the foundational truths in chapters 1 through 10. The principles laid out in parts 1 and 2 of this book give you the biblical motivation behind the components of the ministry laid out in chapters 11 and 12.

If you implement the outline of an orphan ministry without understanding how God is glorified through it, you are not engaging in ministry for the right reasons. Make sure you understand the theology laid out in the previous chapters before implementing the ideas presented in this section.

This third and final section is designed to be a practical guide to beginning or improving an orphan ministry in your church. It focuses on ways in which you may decide to implement the biblical principles that have been discussed in parts 1 and 2.

11 The Components *of a* Church's Orphan Ministry

Whitney and I often find it amusing how unique each of our children is. A woman once stopped my wife and asked her if she was babysitting Ellie. Whitney politely replied that Ellie was adopted. The woman looked at our other three children and saw a boy with dark brown hair, a boy with blonde hair, and a red-headed girl. "Goodness!" she said. "How many children have you adopted?"

Their differences don't stop at hair color. Each of our four children is wildly different, and we enjoy the challenge of meeting their individual needs. Our parenting strategy for one child is different from our strategy for another child. Similarly, your church is vastly different from my church. Therefore, the features of the ministries described in this and the following chapter are not meant to be used as a blueprint for how to do your orphan care ministry. Rather, they are meant to show some possible ways to care for orphans. It will be your task to determine what will and will not be effective in your own ministry context.

Determining Your Church's Ability

There are things the local church can do to care for orphans that no other organization can do. As we saw in chapter 9, for instance, the local church has the unique ability to welcome a child into a community. At the same time, a church can sometimes fail to use its resources wisely, replicating work that has been done more efficiently elsewhere. As a church considers what components will make up its orphan care ministry, it is important that it find the right balance and focus for ministry.

Not Too Much

A church should not attempt to do more than it has the ability to do. Doing too much may mean simply going beyond the resources available to your church. In the excitement of beginning a new ministry, sometimes a church becomes giddy as it considers potential opportunities. It should carefully consider the assets the Lord has provided and plan accordingly.

Doing too much often means taking on things that are best done by other ministries. The church may wisely decide to use an outside organization to review the finances of couples pursuing adoption, or have an outside organization help handle the fund management.[1] The church may also decide to participate in workshops[2] and conferences[3] hosted by other organizations instead of trying to create their own.

Michael Monroe leads Tapestry Ministries at Irving Bible Church in the Dallas area. He notes that oftentimes a church feels as if it needs to develop all its own materials. "For example, it seems that every church wants to develop its own detailed process for everything. That has been done so many times. The church would do better to focus on those areas where it can uniquely serve."[4]

Doing too much may also mean presenting too many opportunities to the congregation too quickly. Greg Buzek, who works with Grace Chapel's orphan ministry in Franklin, Tennessee, says this was a problem at their church: "The biggest mistake we made when we launched our ministry was attempting to do too much. We gave people thirteen ministry areas and they were overwhelmed."[5] As a result, the church had some difficulty raising up and training leaders in some of these areas. Grace Chapel's issue was not that the identified areas for ministry were inappropriate, but rather that the sheer number of them prevented the church from focusing on doing a few things well.

Not Too Little

At the same time, the church should heavily invest in those ministries that it does well. Only the church can provide what is necessary for

---

1. Our church works with Lifesong for Orphans (www.lifesongfororphans.org). Another great organization is the Abba Fund (www.abbafund.org).
2. FamilyLife's *Hope for Orphans* puts on a one-day event entitled *Your Church and the Orphan* that can be very helpful in beginning your ministry (www.hopefororphans.org).
3. The largest evangelical conferences are the Summit conferences, hosted by Christian Alliance for Orphans (http://www.christian-alliance-for-orphans.org/). Another excellent conference is hosted by Together for Adoption (www.togetherforadoption.org).
4. This and subsequent comments from Monroe are from a conversation with the author, November 25, 2009.
5. This and subsequent comments from Buzek are from an email to author, December 23, 2009.

believers to effectively minister to the orphans. Monroe argues that the church, while needing to utilize parachurch organizations, must be careful not to outsource ministry. "Don't give away ministries that the church needs to reclaim."

Monroe also urges churches to carefully consider the difference between *wants* and *needs*: "Many people have a very clear idea of what they want to begin their orphan ministry. If they don't get those elements, they feel as though they can't really begin. That is a bad idea. They already have all that they need to begin the ministry, just not everything they want. These are people who sometimes want the senior pastor to personally come over to their house, start the ministry, and be their best friend. Don't wait to meet the needs of orphans just because you don't have everything that you want for your ministry yet."

Just Right

Deciding what you want your ministry to do will help determine its focus. The key is to find a good balance—not too much and not too little—wisely utilizing the gifts God has provided your church.

Grace Community Church in San Valley, California

Dr. John MacArthur began pastoring Grace Community Church in February 1969. Over the past forty years, the church has experienced phenomenal growth and today it ministers to thousands of people on Sunday mornings. Millions more are reached through their radio ministry, conferences, and the seminary and college associated with the church. Grace Community is a church that is passionate about God's Word and extremely influential in the evangelical community. As a large church, they have access to resources many smaller churches do not.

Grace Community has cared for orphans in a variety of ways over the years. When he first began his pastorate, Dr. MacArthur would go to hospitals and minister to women who were transferring the parental rights of their newborns. Missionaries from the church have engaged in meeting the needs of the fatherless and numerous families at Grace have been actively engaged in adopting and fostering.

But it was only in 2009 that an official orphan ministry began. In November, the church launched "Hands of Hope" and held a fair with various Christian agencies. Forty families signed up to participate in the ministry the first day. The ministry's initial focus was on equipping through their teaching ministry and encouraging participation in the foster care system.

Grace Community is also working hard to integrate orphan care ministry into the overall life of their church. Dr. Mark Tatlock, who helps oversee Hands for Hope at Grace, was impressed with how hard the children's ministry worked to meet the needs of at-risk kids. "They trained the ministry staff so that they would be aware of issues that might come up with children from the foster care system and how they should respond. They were diligent to welcome children into the life of the church."[6]

Tatlock sees the church playing a crucial role in supporting parents who work with orphans. "One thing we are doing is helping develop counseling resources for at-risk kids once they get into our homes. We think this will be helpful both to parents and to missionaries working in the field." Since many churches struggle to help parents who have adopted, there is a need for continued growth for orphan care ministries as they seek to "mature in the area of knowing how to incorporate children and provide resources for their parents."

The orphan care ministry at Grace is led by the pastoral staff, but the nuts and bolts of the ministry is carried out by lay leaders. Adoption awareness was raised at the leadership level when several men on the pastoral staff adopted at the same time. The elders were able to experience the highs and lows of their adoption journeys and see the value in the orphan care ministry.

Yet even at a church with leadership solidly behind the ministry and large enough to have significant resources, there is a need to take things slowly. While Grace Community is excited about what God has done thus far in their church, they look forward to continuing to expand their care to orphans. Future projects include establishing a matching grant fund for adopting families and developing training resources.

Tapestry in Irving, Texas

Irving Bible Church has an "outside-the-church-walls" ministry philosophy. This means that much of their ministry is outreach focused. Tapestry is obviously influenced by this philosophy and tries to focus on the needs of those outside their church. In the past several years, the ministry has grown from serving 20 adults to more than 1,100 adults, plus countless children. Of the 1,100 adults who are being served by at least one of Tapestry's ministries, fewer than 200 are from their own church. Several hundred have no church affiliation and the rest come from more than 100 other churches in the Dallas-Fort Worth area.

Monroe says that their goal is to connect people in their adoption journey. "If we have a special event and only two people show up, we don't

---

6. This and subsequent comments from Tatlock are from a phone interview with the author, March 9, 2010.

get worried and cancel it. We see it as useful for those two people." Their monthly events are "not heavy on spiritual stuff or theology, though that is certainly a focus. We try to weave in faith stories—how God is at work in many different ways in the adoption or foster care journey."

This philosophy of ministry is very different from our church's philosophy. While our church would agree that theology must be practical, we also believe theology is indispensable for properly preparing saints to engage in caring for orphans. Our events do often contain a time of teaching. It might be hard for three hundred people who are not part of a church to find our church's orphan care ministry appealing.

There are, however, some valuable things our church can learn from Tapestry's ministry. First, we need to see the evangelism opportunities inherent in orphan care ministry. Tapestry is reaching a segment of the population that we simply are not. If it is true that orphan care ministry allows us to proclaim the gospel, a church needs to capitalize on that.

Second, Tapestry has a focus on the larger body of Christ that is encouraging. For example, they noticed that there are many Christian couples chasing the same financial aid. "Many financial assistance organizations have a 3-to-1 turn-down ratio, meaning that only one couple of every three that apply receive financial assistance for their adoption. At the same time, you have churches that are not moving the money that is in their funds. They have fifty thousand to two-hundred-thousand-dollar balances when really the goal should be to have a zero balance," Monroe notes. Tapestry, together with Lifesong for Orphans, is organizing a "fund of funds" where different churches can share the resources that God has entrusted to them.

Third, Tapestry is focused on practical training, meeting the real needs that individuals have. Monroe expresses a frustration with ministries that are heavy on theology but never offer any application to life. He challenges churches to ask what needs they are meeting with their ministries. It is vital that our theology impact lives.

Grace Chapel in Leiper's Fork, Tennessee

Grace Chapel began their ministry in July 2008 and launched publically in early 2009. As mentioned earlier, they quickly realized they had taken on too much and reevaluated their ministry goals. Buzek says that their church now focuses on three initiatives. "Our ministry's primary goals are to (1) engage the people in short term missions trips to aid orphans, (2) help people who want to adopt go through the process and get support, and (3) launch Safe Families, which is a positive alternative to the state child foster system, allowing at-risk parents to work out their problems without having to worry about losing custody of their kids." As a result, the church has seen the Lord work in some great ways as children have been brought into homes through adoption and the church has participated in joyfully caring for the orphan.

Bethany Community Church in Washington, Illinois
        You have already heard quite a bit about our ministry throughout the book. The church that I pastor was planted by Bethany Baptist Church, where I served as an associate pastor. It was in my capacity as an associate pastor that I helped begin the orphan ministry there. When we planted Bethany Community, we did not try to recreate an orphan ministry but continued to partner with our parent church. Bethany Community is a church of between four and five hundred. We do not have all the resources of a mega-church, but we make up for that by partnering with Bethany Baptist Church and Living Hope Community Church.

        The ministry at our church is constantly evolving as God stirs the hearts of his saints. Sometimes there are many families adopting internationally. At other times, it seems we have more pursuing domestic adoptions or being called to foster. Depending upon what God is doing in the lives of the saints, our ministry can look very different from one month to the next.

Your Church
        Your orphan ministry's final "look" will be determined by factors that are distinctive to your church. You will have to decide how best to implement the biblical principles in your context. This chapter and the following chapter contain some suggestions. I would encourage you not to try to reproduce a ministry but rather to learn from the successes and failures of others. I would also offer this nugget for what it is worth: Our most effective ministries have been those that we tailor-made to fit our church; our least effective ministries have been those where we tried to reproduce what another church was doing.

Beginning the Ministry

        The following are some suggested steps to beginning your church's orphan ministry. The purpose of this book is not to lay out a step-by-step process of how to start a church orphans ministry but rather give you an overview of some suggested steps. When our church ministry was starting, we used some material from Hope for Orphans®, a ministry of FamilyLife®, as we brainstormed what our ministry might look like. Currently, Hope for Orphans has developed an eight-step process for starting a church orphans ministry. This process is detailed in the book *Launching an Orphans Ministry in Your Church* (FamilyLife, 2006) and is presented in a live workshop entitled "Your Church and the Orphan." Your church may find it beneficial to host a workshop for your church and other churches in the area.[7]

Here are some suggested first steps as you begin your orphan ministry. While I have tried to lay them out in a generally chronological format, there is a lot of overlap, and the order in which you proceed may vary from the one described here.

Consider the Biblical Principles

The first step in beginning your orphan care ministry is to expose yourself and your church to the biblical principles that shape our theological understanding of the fatherless. Obviously, I happen to think that this book is an excellent tool for this task. Think through these principles carefully yourself and help others think through them as well.[8]

If there are already individuals in your church who are passionate about beginning an orphan ministry, it might be good to go through this book or something similar with them before going further. Going through parts 1 and 2 of this study will help ensure that there is oneness of understanding concerning the nature and purpose of the church and orphans. Going through part 3 together can help you as you try to finalize the ministry you believe the Lord is preparing for your church.

Contact Parachurch Organizations

A useful next step is to contact evangelical parachurch organizations that work at equipping churches to care for orphans. Several of these organizations have been referred to already in this book. Christian Alliance for Orphans serves as a hub for the evangelical church and its orphan ministries. Its stated aim is to "ignite and equip individuals and churches for effective, Christ-honoring service to orphans."[9] Most of the major evangelical orphan ministries are members of the alliance. All of them must subscribe to a solid, evangelical doctrinal statement and are held to high

---

7. If you need more information than what you find here, Hope for Orphans (www.hopefororphans.org), a ministry of FamilyLife, assists churches in beginning orphan ministries.

8. Together for Adoption (www.togetherforadoption.org) has many helpful resources for churches desiring to increase their theological understanding of adoption.

9. Christian Alliance for Orphans, http://christian-alliance-for-orphans.org/component/content/category/1-about (accessed December 2, 2010).

standards of financial accountability. Their annual conference is an excellent resource for gaining exposure to various orphan ministries.

As you consider how to handle the financial side of the ministry, Lifesong for Orphans is a parachurch organization that can be helpful. Along with creating indigenous orphan care solutions in several African, European, and Latin American countries, Lifesong creates adoption funding solutions. Andy Lehman, vice president of Lifesong, was instrumental in helping our own orphan ministry get started.

Hope for Orphans is a division of FamilyLife ministries and works to equip the church to care for orphans. Their focus is on helping the church with many of the practical elements of orphan care ministry.

Research Other Churches

It was helpful for our church to see how orphan care ministries had been implemented in other churches, especially churches of a similar size with a similar ministry philosophy. At this point, having a contact person at a parachurch organization was beneficial because the parachurch organization could connect us with other churches. As the committee or elders at our church had questions regarding the direction or implementation of the ministry, we would often contact the leaders at other churches and ask how they had dealt with a particular issue. Their insights gave us the ability to make new mistakes instead of repeating old ones.

Approach the Church Leaders

Before proceeding too far, you should at least informally discuss the ministry with the church leaders. If there is going to be strong opposition to an aspect of the ministry, it is better to know that now rather than later. If there is a staff member at the church who has already been thinking about beginning this ministry, it would be a helpful to get that person's input at an early stage in the process.

I would recommend getting together with someone in church leadership over breakfast or lunch and discussing what God has been laying on your heart. Present the possible ministry in very broad terms and mention that you will have a formal proposal in the future. Because of your research to this point, you should be able to answer any big questions and know where to find the answers to questions you might not have thought of already.

It may also be helpful to mention that you are not currently asking for anything—which means there is nothing for them to say no to! You are simply beginning a dialogue. It may even be a good idea to graciously offer some sort of gift . . . such as a fine book on orphan care ministry.

Consider the Components of Your Orphan Care Ministry

Ideally, you have already identified a core group that is going to be providing leadership to the ministry. This group should begin brainstorming different ways that the church might be able to care for the fatherless. They can consider various ministry opportunities, such as:

- praying for orphans and those ministering to them
- adopting domestically or internationally
- sponsoring orphans
- financially supporting couples who are adopting
- participating in mission trips
- offering biblical counseling
- fostering a child
- fellowshipping with other orphan advocates,
- assisting with administrative duties
- helping with communication

Finalize and Present a Proposal

Through the prayerful process of research and brainstorming, how God has gifted your church to care for the fatherless should become clearer. This is the time when you should begin finalizing the proposal you will present to the leadership. The end of this chapter contains a sample outline of a ministry proposal.

The goal of presenting a proposal is not simply to get the leaders's approval. Rather, the primary purpose is to give the leaders a vision for the ministry and allow them to help shape the final product. If at the end of your time with the leaders, they are generally supportive of the plan in its current state—fantastic. But it is far more important to help the leaders gain a vision for the ministry and get direction from them than to have them rubber stamp a proposal.

Again, remember that you have been thinking about orphan care ministry for some time. It may be a new idea to the leaders at your church, so be patient and give them time to let your proposal sink in.

Establish a Leadership Committee

Establishing a leadership committee could take place at various stages in the process, depending upon the support you have from your church. The purpose of this committee is to divide up the responsibilities of the ministry and advance its goals. It is helpful, therefore, to have people on the committee with a wide array of backgrounds. If your ministry is planning on ministering through foster care, domestic adoptions, international adoptions, and mission trips, it would be helpful to have people who have backgrounds in each of those areas on your ministry team.

Communicate the New Ministry to the Church

Lehman offers several suggestions for those who are beginning a new orphan ministry that I think should be considered before presenting it to the church body.[10] (1) Do not create a guilt complex—even implicitly. Just because you have cared for orphans does not mean that others are called to do so in the same way. We can sometimes unintentionally imply that. As you present the ministry, let people see the joy of participating in caring for the fatherless. (2) You probably do not want to use the word "adoption" in the title of your ministry, since that could pigeonhole your ministry. If it is true that God calls the church as a whole to minister to the orphan, then it is important to help the whole body see the ways in which they can fit into the ministry. (3) Make sure you show how ministry to the fatherless is already happening within the church. Most likely, orphan care is not going to be a completely new endeavor for your church. People just do not know where it is taking place and need to be made aware of it.

One way to do this is by having an Orphan Sunday. Many churches choose to highlight their orphan ministries on a Sunday in November, which is National Adoption Month. The advantage of observing Orphan Sunday in November is that people in your church are more likely to hear a program on the radio or read an article about orphan ministry during this time. Though there is something special about participating at the same time as other churches, the important thing is to have some time that is regularly set aside to draw attention to the plight of the fatherless. Due to existing ministry commitments during the month of November, our church highlights the orphan care ministry on Sanctity of Life Sunday in January.

An Orphan Sunday should communicate to the church what the ministry is and why believers should be excited about it. The purpose is not to guilt people or manipulate their emotions but to help them develop a passion to see God glorified through this new ministry.

Orphan Sunday at our church is a time of celebration, and several people have told me it is their favorite Sunday of the year. The service consists of several elements: there are recorded testimonies of individuals who have been involved in caring for orphans; the sermon focuses on the sanctity of life, with orphan care being a primary application; and we try to have specific, focused ministry opportunities to which people can respond.

---

10. From an interview with author, November 20, 2009.

Monroe views the participation of people in the church like an inverted pyramid. "Realistically, at the very tip of the pyramid, at best 5 percent are going to consider fostering or adopting or going on a mission trip. The question for us on a Sunday when we have the opportunity to present our ministry is, How do we reach the bigger section of the pyramid?"

On a recent Orphan Sunday, for example, Tapestry offered five ways for members of the congregation to respond. They could (1) purchase a Bible in the foyer for $10, and then a Christian foster agency would give those Bibles to children in foster care; (2) sign up to pray for a child in the foster system; (3) volunteer as an advocate for children in foster care; (4) become a mentor for foster youth; or (5) become an adoptive or foster family.

For your church's first Orphan Sunday, it may be helpful to invite people to a luncheon after church that will help introduce and explain the ministry. At this meeting, an overview of the ministry can be presented more fully and questions can be answered.

Begin Orphan Study

It should be no surprise that I believe having an orphan Bible study is a crucial component to the success of your ministry. There needs to be a time when those who would consider caring for the orphan are helped to understand how to do this ministry biblically.

Remember that your goal is not merely to get kids provided for physically. Your goal is to motivate the saints to do the right thing for the right reason—that God would be glorified in our lives, in our churches, and in the life of the orphan.

Some of the material we used when we began our ministry had several limitations. First, it had a narrow focus: couples who were adopting. Second, it did not provide the in-depth Bible study that I felt was necessary for couples and individuals who were going to invest their lives in caring for the orphan. This book is the result of the supplemental material I began to develop for our church's orphan study.

The orphan study does several things. First and foremost, it helps you know what you are to do and why. Second, it provides a natural filter for your ministry—especially those who might consider adopting and asking the church for resources. If a couple is unwilling to make the time commitment to attend the study, it may—though not necessarily—provide some insight into their spiritual maturity. Third, if led well, the study can help people deal with many issues that go beyond the scope of the material covered in the study. Fourth, it provides a community of folks who are able to encourage and motivate one another.

Continuing Orphan Care Ministry

It is difficult to launch an orphan ministry and difficult to maintain it. Lehman suggests that you think of creative ways to keep the ministry in front of the congregation: "It is important to continue to celebrate milestones. Sometimes, a ministry begins with a big push, then they just never mention it again and it fizzles out. Or they roll it out once a year: here's the orphan ministry! Some churches are able to maintain the ministry, and other churches need help. The churches that do well keep the ministry before the congregation in a variety of ways, such as giving testimonies when children come home or even commissioning parents who are adopting internationally before they leave."

The church should continually be teaching on the needs of the disenfranchised. It should also be prepared to plug people into ministry as the Holy Spirit works in their lives. Monroe says that when the Tapestry ministry presented the five ways to respond on an Orphan Sunday, a woman came up with a sixth way following one of the services. She asked if she could start a kid's closet where people could donate diapers, clothing, and toys for children. Though this had not been an area of ministry they were considering, Tapestry encouraged her to do so and helped her get it started. This ministry effort is extremely successful today. If their ministry were not flexible, they would not have been able to adapt when people were led in new directions.

Sample Outline of Ministry Proposal[11]

I. Ministry Goal
   Equip believers to reach foster children and orphans with the guidance, support and prayer of the church body—to the glory of God![12]

II. Biblical Mandates
   A. The uniqueness of Christian orphan care[13]
   B. Compassion, the disenfranchised, and the orphan[14]

---

11. The original Open Hearts, Open Homes ministry proposal was prepared for Bethany Baptist Church by Dan Hawkinson (May 28, 2006). It has been slightly modified.
12. The ministry's goal is intentionally broad.
13. See chapter 1.
14. See chapter 2. We could include much of the information from part 1 in the

1. The problem of passionless compassion
2. God has compassion for the disenfranchised
   a. God is a compassionate God (Exod. 33:19)
   b. Orphans are one of the groups that receive God's special compassion (Exod. 22:21–27; Deut. 10:18a; Pss. 10:14b; 68:5; Hos. 14:3)
3. God's people are to have compassion for the disenfranchised
   a. The necessity of biblical compassion in the life of a believer (Luke 10:25–37)
   b. God's people are to have compassion for the orphan (Isa. 1:17; James 1:27)
4. True compassion is fueled by a passion for God to be worshipped (Matt. 9:35–38)

III. Opportunities for Believers at Bethany[15]
   A. Domestic adoption: Sharing the love of Christ with a child by making him or her a permanent member of a family
      1. Agency adoption: Children matched with parents via agencies (Department of Children and Family Services [DCFS], Catholic or Lutheran Social Services)
      2. Private adoption: Children matched with parents via doctor, lawyer, crisis pregnancy center, word of mouth, etc.
   B. International adoption: Sharing the love of Christ with a child from another country by making him or her a permanent member of a family
      1. The number of orphans worldwide is more than one hundred million
      2. Common countries for adopting in 2005 include China, Russia, Ukraine, Vietnam, India, and Guatemala
      3. Children matched with parents via agencies
      4. Agency has staff in both the United States and in target country
      5. Parachurch organizations can help recommend agencies

---

proposal, but it is probably most helpful to focus on the first two chapters in the initial presentation. It might be wise to give the leadership some material prior to meeting with them so that they can mull over the biblical mandates prior to hearing your proposal.

15. In this section, we lay out the ways we believe our church can be involved in caring for orphans. Notice definitions are offered to help people understand terms. For example, many on a leadership team will have no idea what is involved in an international adoption and how it works.

C. Foster care: Sharing the love of Christ with children by bringing them into the family on a short- or long-term basis
  1. Short term foster opportunities exist for families to offer respite to long-term families
  2. Eligible children range from newborn to age 18
  3. Through the Illinois DCFS, families must complete a home study and classes
  4. There is a constant waiting list of children
  5. Families can decide to foster a "placement" child based on gender, race, age, disability, likelihood of adoption, and any other available information
D. Mentoring: Guiding a family through the adoption and foster process from the very first step
  1. Many families within Bethany have experienced adopting and/or fostering and can offer prayers, advice, answers, encouragement, and guidance to new families
  2. Adopting and fostering can be emotionally and mentally overwhelming
E. Prayer: Praying for orphans and those who are ministering to them
  1. The faithful prayers of believers at Bethany will be essential for this ministry
  2. Prayer needs include:
     a. Families both considering and in the process of adopting and fostering
     b. Children who will be impacted by this ministry
     c. Orphanages around the world that sustain children while they wait for adoption
F. Financial support: Giving to help meet the needs of caring for orphans, specifically the costs associated with adoption[16]
  1. Believers at Bethany have the opportunity to give to help meet the financial needs associated with adoption
  2. Adoption expenses range from $10,000 to $30,000
  3. Opportunities may exist for:
     a. Giving to specific families who are trying to adopt
     b. Giving toward an adoption fund
     c. Giving to the general fund
G. Babysitting: Providing relief to adoptive and foster parents by babysitting[17]

---

16. Chapter 12 will deal with the financial aspect of adoption in greater detail.
17. When you initially plan your ministry, it is probable that some of the things

H. Administration and technology: Assisting Open Hearts, Open Homes by organizing, planning, and communicating for the ministry
 1. Communication to the church and those involved
 2. Planning and running events
 3. Answering questions
 4. Leadership responsibilities for specific areas
I. Mission trips

IV. Opportunities for the Church
 A. Facilities: Utilizing the church building and resources to support orphan care ministries
  1. Informational luncheons several times a year
  2. Meeting place for Bible study
  3. Babysitting team once a month or quarterly for participating families
  4. Provide a meeting place for DCFS training classes
  5. Meetings for general administration purposes
 B. Communication: Helping the Open Hearts, Open Homes ministry communicate to the body
 C. Financial: Assisting the orphan care ministry through monetary aid[18]
  1. The need: Expenses can range in cost from $10,000 to $30,000, varying significantly based on country, agency and foreign vs. domestic. Most significant expenses consist of:
   a. Agency/Program fees: $2,000–$28,000
   b. Orphanage fees or donations: $1,000–$5,000
   c. Travel—airfare & accommodations: $500–$10,000
   d. Attorney fees: $500–$9,500
   e. Birthmother expenses: $0–$5,000
   f. Home study fees: $500–$3,000
   g. Document fees: $35–$2,400
   h. Misc: $500–$5,000 (screening, fees in foreign country, physicals, dossier translation & preparation, USCIS fees, etc.)
  2. Existing help

---

you suggest will never materialize. This area has been one of the areas that has never materialized for us in a formal way, though it certainly occurs informally.

18. When churches balk, it is often because of the dollar signs. It is important that you are up-front with the leaders regarding how fees work and what fees are reasonable.

a. Employer grants
b. Lifesong for Orphans
c. Adoption tax credit
3. Proposed funding plan for Bethany: Allow individuals or families to contribute to providing for orphans, primarily through helping fund adoptions
   a. Adoption fund: Establish an adoption fund that gives financial aid to members of the church[19] with the amount given based on need. This fund will be maintained through special giving and will not be a line item in the church budget.[20]
   b. General Fund: The orphan ministry will receive funding from the general church budget on an annual basis. These funds will go toward administrative and other miscellaneous ministry expenses.
   c. Support letters: Similar in concept to support letters for mission trips, these letters will be sent out by members of our church who are adopting, to friends and family members who may wish to assist them in their adoption. Funds received from these letters will go to the adoption fund.
   d. Special gifts: The church may also decide to give special gifts[21] to families who are adopting. These special gifts would be

---

19. Our church began by making the decision to restrict financial aid to members of the church initially. We believed our primary responsibility was to members of our own body. As God has grown our ministry, we are reconsidering how we can assist the larger body of Christ. This is an example of starting small with what you can handle.

20. The church still budgeted for our ministry (see next item), but we created a special fund that people could give to so that 100 percent of donated expenses would go directly to providing for adoptions. The ministry essentially has two funds. One fund is a fund that people give to and all the proceeds go to caring for orphans. The other fund is funded by the general giving to the church. This second fund appears as a line item in our church budget, and we draw from it when there are any other expenses like sending someone to a conference or paying for administrative needs.

21. These gifts are what some call "interest-free loans," but that is not what they are technically. A person who receives these gifts is under no legal obligation to pay them back. Currently, families who adopt can receive adoption tax credits over a five-year time period. These gifts from the church are given and couples commit to pay the church back the gift as they receive that credit. See chapter 12 for more details.

funded from memorial funds and based upon how much a family will receive from the adoption tax credit.

e. Consider starting a fund at Lifesong for their matching grant program.[22] Grant amount is needs based at the discretion of Lifesong.

f. Funds provided by Bethany should have specific criteria established by leadership
Criteria examples: married for at least a year, members of Bethany, completed the Bible study, personal financial status review, clear articulation of the gospel.

V. Needed from leadership and next steps[23]

A. Continued direction from leadership
B. Organization of ministry participants into functional areas (domestic and foreign adoption, foster care)
C. Plan Bible study and informational meetings
D. Finalize scope of the ministry at Bethany and begin communicating

Pausing for Breath

I trust that the Lord is going to do wonderful things in the life of your church as you seek to be faithful to care for the fatherless. As we saw in chapter 9, the gifts of the Holy Spirit are varied. The way he moves in one church will be different than the way he moves in another. Hopefully, this chapter has gotten your creative juices flowing and you can begin to move forward with a God-honoring plan.

---

22. Ultimately, we decided not to keep our fund at Lifesong, but instead to administer our own fund. There are advantages to each, but unless you have people who are well-versed in church financial laws and gifted administratively, I would recommend using Lifesong for Orphans or another ministry such as Abba Fund.

23. It is helpful to let the leaders know where you are headed and give them the opportunity to provide direction. There are some specific requests here that allow the leaders to feel involved, but also enough detail has been laid out to where they may feel comfortable allowing you to proceed.

12 The Components of a Church's Adoption Ministry

*O*ur *orphan care ministry team* has tried, but it's really hard. No matter how often we remind ourselves that we are an orphan ministry, we still refer to the ministry as "the adoption ministry."

Throughout the book, it has been my goal to emphasize orphan care ministry as a whole, but as much as we want to highlight the need to participate in other ministries like foster care and mission trips, the act of bringing a child into their "forever family" is so powerful that it almost eclipses other ministries to the fatherless.[1] When most people in our church think about the orphan ministry, they think "adoption." They pray for families pursuing adoption, they greet adopted children at the airport when they come home, they see them dedicated, and they minister to them in Sunday school classes.

Adoption is a crucial part of a church's orphan ministry and the part of the orphan ministry that most people in the church will notice and think about. Due to its importance in the life of the church, this chapter will cover four things that are important for the church to provide for couples who are adopting: biblical instruction, accountability, financial assistance, and ongoing support.

Provide Biblical Instruction

Imagine that your orphan ministry experiences incredible success the first few years of its existence. Countless hours and tens of thousands of

---

1. When I first saw someone use the phrase "forever family," it was on an adoption announcement. The announcement contained the child's name, date of birth, and the date they were "brought into their forever family." I thought the announcement was telling me that the child had died! I now understand the term and appreciate what it is trying to communicate, but it is a good example of how orphan advocates have their own lingo.

dollars are invested in it. Powerful, tangible results are seen. Children are brought into homes, suffering is alleviated, and the church is seen as a beacon of hope in the evangelical community. How terrible would it be to find out in eternity that all your work was useless?

This truth is the heart of this book: orphan care ministry must be biblically informed and motivated by the desire to worship God. Point your people first not to the orphan but to God. As they learn about him and come to love him, care for the orphan is inevitable.

Provide Accountability

Your ministry must be prepared for an eventuality that you may someday have to face. At some point in time you may have to tell a family that you do not believe they are prepared to adopt a child even though they have their hearts set on it. This may be the most difficult part of the ministry. The inescapable truth of the matter is that not everyone is prepared to adopt a child and train them to know and worship the Lord.

There are many reasons why it is necessary to provide accountability. First, accountability is necessary *for the protection of the child.* Your church is helping bring this child into a family and has a responsibility to him or her. Second, accountability is necessary *for the protection of the church.* A great deal of money can potentially flow through the church as it strives to care for orphans. The money is God's and has been entrusted to the church to use for his purposes. If that resource is used wisely, it can have tremendous potential to glorify God. If it is used poorly, the church will be accountable to the Lord for our poor stewardship. Third, accountability is *for the sake of the family who is adopting.* Your counsel to a couple who is not prepared to adopt will help them as they grow in their walk with the Lord. "Faithful are the wounds of a friend," Proverbs 27:6 tells us. The response of an individual or couple to godly correction says much about their spiritual maturity.

Agencies

As the church provides accountability, it relies upon other organizations to aid it in that task. It is a relatively safe assumption that if a couple is adopting through a reputable agency, that agency is providing some of the needed accountability. Children are (usually!) not just handed out randomly to families with cash. There are screening processes that the agency and other various government entities will conduct.

Therefore, one area of accountability is ensuring that couples use reputable agencies. Recently, someone contacted our ministry and asked that we pass on some information on potential adoptions from an adoption attorney. We asked a local attorney to review his fee structure and methodology and concluded that his fees were too high. We were uncomfortable supporting people who utilized his services. In this way, we believe the church can protect God's resources and help steer families to agencies with stellar reputations.

Bible Study

Requiring couples who are considering adopting to go attend a Bible study is another way to provide accountability. The study should be a prerequisite to supporting a family in their adoption efforts. At our church, the Bible study serves as the entry point into our adoption ministry. Everyone who receives financial assistance from our ministry has been through it.

A small group Bible study is a remarkably effective way to allow people to discern their readiness and potentially opt out of adopting on their own. A person may go through the study and realize that there are idols in their heart they need to work through before proceeding further. A couple may realize that God is calling them to a far different ministry than they had originally anticipated. The Bible study forces couples to answer questions they might not ever have considered on their own. It also helps develop relationships that are going to be crucial to helping them through some potentially difficult times after the adoption is finalized.

Application Process

There may be several aspects of your ministry that are open to anyone. A person could receive prayer, access resource materials, or utilize the counseling ministry without formally becoming a part of the ministry. But those who want to officially participate in the ministry and receive financial aid should go through an application process. That application process begins with filling out a packet. I have included a sample of the packet our church uses (which was adapted from Lifesong's packet) in the appendix (see p. 207).

Reviewing the Application

Because we rely on Lifesong for Orphans to review the financial aspects of the couple's application, the pages titled "Net Worth" (p. 212) and "Cash Flow" (p. 213) are not submitted to the church, but directly to Lifesong, along with the applicant's most current year's federal tax return (1040 form). Lifesong then reviews the applicant's finances and recommends to

Bethany Community Church what amount to grant and/or give as a no-interest loan based upon financial need (see "Provide Financial Assistance" below).

While that is going on, the orphan committee leadership team reviews the rest of the application and makes note of any areas that need clarification or that we would like to discuss.

Interviews

The next step is to schedule a time for the orphan ministry committee to interview the couple. Our first interviews were somewhat humorous. We were all so enthralled by the fact that people were adopting in our church that the "interview" consisted of a forty-five minute to an hour conversation where we talked about how excited we were for the couple. We never asked the hard questions that needed to be asked of them. We soon realized what we were doing and began to prepare for the interviews better. We listed areas we wanted to make certain we covered based on the application such as the couple's personal salvation testimony, the health of their marriage, their parenting philosophy, and their ability to understand and articulate the gospel.

Following the interview, the committee discusses any concerns or further questions we might have for the couple. If there are no concerns, we recommend the couple to the elders for approval. The elders then approve the couple to be officially supported by the church. We send a letter to the couple letting them know of the elders' decision and our excitement for their calling to the ministry.

Provide Financial Assistance[2]

Providing financial assistance can be a confusing undertaking and one with legal ramifications. Here are some of the things we do as we try to help families.

Overview

We provide financial assistance to families who are adopting because

---

2. The following pages do not contain legal advice. I would encourage you to contact an attorney or look through relevant IRS tax code. I am a pastor-teacher not an accountant or an attorney. I cannot adequately deal with legal questions though I can confirm that, theologically speaking, the IRS is soulless.

we believe the entire church should participate in bringing children home. As we saw in chapter 9, the church is a family, and each part works together in order to do ministry. Many who are called to adopt do not have the tens of thousands of dollars required to bring a child home. Similarly, many who could financially afford the cost of an adoption may not be at a position in life where they can bring a child into their home. One of the orphan ministry's goals is to connect givers with those in need.

Practical Guidelines

The general model for our adoption funding is based upon a process designed by our missions committee for short-term mission trips. Financial resources are acquired from three primary sources: the adopting family, the church, and those who wish to give special support.

Family's Resources

The first source, the family, consists of funds the family has at their disposal. The application they fill out contains a section in which the family describes what resources they feel they can realistically contribute to an adoption. Sometimes, a family will put in a very high number that is not realistic. They are taking into consideration every single asset at their disposal (i.e., taking out a second mortgage, cashing out their 401k, etc). I often encourage couples to allow the church and their family and friends to try and assist them more, if possible. It may be that we are unable to meet their need and so it will become necessary to take some radical steps. But if the church can come alongside a family and keep them from debt that could hinder their future kingdom work, that seems far more preferable.

On the other hand, it is important to make sure that a couple has personally invested in their own adoption ministry. If they are completely reliant upon other people and the church to finance their adoption, then they have possibly missed a vision for sacrifice that would be beneficial for their spiritual health. Most organizations wait to receive applications for financial assistance until after a home study has been completed to ensure that the couple is investing personally in this ministry. Your church may wish to consider doing the same.

Obviously, figuring out how much a couple should be able to give is a little tricky. It is even more so when you are talking about the finances of your friends in the church. For this reason, we do not even deal with these questions as a committee. All of this is outsourced to Lifesong for Orphans, who can more objectively evaluate, based upon a variety of criteria, what the capability of a family should be.

The Church

The second source from which the funding for an adoption comes is the church. We believe that it is important for every person who tithes at our church to have a sense that they are participating in the orphan care ministry. Therefore, we offer a grant to families from our church who are adopting. Lifesong determines the amount of these grants to help the church avoid even an appearance of favoritism.

Some organizations refer to these as "matching grants," but I am somewhat ambivalent on that term. First, we plan on giving those funds no matter what others do, so it is not entirely accurate to call them "matching." Second, I want to be careful how we motivate people. I want them to give regardless of what other people are doing. Others disagree and rightly point out that offering a matching grant helps excite people as they see God double their gifts.

Another way in which the church assists couples with their financial needs is by giving what are often called "interest-free loans." This term reflects what practically takes place, but the transaction is not really a loan. The church is not a bank and does not give loans—interest-free or otherwise. What we do is give money to couples based upon how much money they will receive from the federal adoption tax-credit. Lifesong evaluates their tax returns to estimate how much benefit the family will receive from this tax credit. The church then gives the couple this amount, and they agree to pay it back to the church over the following years as they receive their adoption tax credit. The purpose of this is to allow couples to avoid going into debt and to maximize the resources the federal government offers.

Support Raising

The third source of funding for an adoption comes from support raising. Families and friends are offered the opportunity to give to a fund from which we will offer further assistance, usually based upon the amount that is raised by that family. It is important to follow IRS guidelines in designated giving. My interpretation of current tax code is that the church can allow people to indicate how they wish for their funds to be directed, but the church itself must maintain complete authority over how those funds are used in order for the gifts to be tax deductible. It may use the funds for the suggested purpose or it may not. If a couple has been given more money than they need, for instance, the church might decide to direct the excess funds toward the adoption needs of another family.

The appendix contains examples of the letters that we encourage families who are adopting to send to their friends and family. The first letter

(p. 216) is from the church. It is designed to explain a little bit about our ministry and to legitimize the request for funds. Some people the couple will be sending the letter to have never heard of financially supporting an adoption. Seeing that there is an organization that is receiving the funds—and that their donations are tax deductible—can increase their comfort level. The second letter (p. 217) is from the family and provides the autobiographical details and describes the need.

The Lord has blessed the financial aspect of our ministry immensely. It is a joy to our church and individual believers within it to be able to give to the adoption of children. As a ministry, we do not support fundraisers. We believe it is better to give the members of the church the ability to meet the needs of their brothers and sisters and experience the accompanying eternal rewards.

Provide Ongoing Support

The fourth area of provision for an adoption ministry is emotional and spiritual support. This is an aspect of our ministry that I often do not "get," sometimes to the amused frustration of the female members on our orphan committee. When speaking with adoptive families, they will most often identify the need for ongoing spiritual and emotional support as their biggest struggle. From the beginning of our ministry, when we were dealing with the issue of adoption, we tried to help people think through how tough the path before them could be. No matter how strongly you tell a person who is considering adopting, "This is going to be far more difficult than you can fathom!" all they hear is, "This is going to be the most wonderful experience of your life." Both statements may be true, but one needs to hear both of them.

Now that we are a few years into the ministry, we have adoptive moms and dads who are dealing with the "after the dream comes true" issues.[3] There has been a climactic anticipation for this child to come into their home; now the child is here and instead of loving his new mom and dad, he is ambivalent toward them or, worse, openly antagonistic. Or the new mom struggles because when she looks at her new little girl from China *she feels nothing for her and it scares her out of her mind!*

What the women on our committee recognized early on and what took me some time to grasp is that there is sometimes a need to have a place where adoptive families—especially moms—can share the struggles

---

3. See Gardner, *After the Dream Comes True.*

they are going through. They need an atmosphere where they can be vulnerable and at the same time receive solid, godly counsel from other adoptive parents.

Perhaps because I am not an extremely emotional person, I did not see this as a real need. A few years into the ministry, however, I am convinced that before, during, and after the adoption process, the church needs to provide an environment where moms and dads are provided spiritual care. They need to be able to biblically process the emotionally charged situations they are going through.

There are several ways that a church can create this environment. First, by having a strong prayer ministry, where the church is aware of needs in one another's lives. Second, by having regular, informal times of fellowship with other families. Third, by having a strong biblical counseling ministry that can help people think through their problems and their solutions biblically.

Final Thoughts

This book's thesis is that the church runs the terrible risk of doing the right things for the wrong reason. Your goal is not primarily to get a lot of people in your church feeling really good about themselves by bringing cute little orphan kids into their homes. Your goal is worship. Your overwhelming passion and drive must be to see God glorified in the life of his church as orphans are brought into homes and taught about worship of the Most High God. The families who participate in the orphan ministry need to comprehend the true nature of the task before them. By whatever means necessary, help them understand the glory of God, the reality of suffering, and the bigger picture of the ministry in which they are involved. If you do anything less, your ministry is simply spinning its wheels, not really engaging what God has called the church to do.

I recently reconnected with Ty and Allison, some friends from high school who are a great example of how God uses a variety of ways to call us to minister to the fatherless. When Allison was seventh months pregnant with their first child, Ty walked into their bedroom where she was checking her e-mail. She stood up and turned to face him with a strange look on her face. "It was this mixture of incredible excitement and joy," says Ty. "She's ready to give them to us," Allison exclaimed and Ty knew instantly what she meant.

There were three children who were being cared for by an older woman who was very close with Allison's family. The oldest was ten and the twins were seven. Ty and Allison had been praying for these children for quite some time and now, unexpectedly, this woman was asking for their help. She had realized she could not care for the children, and there was no one else to whom she could turn.

Ty and Allison had many excuses they could have given. They were just about to begin a family of their own. They weren't prepared to instantly become a family of four with a newborn. Their house was too small. There should have been other people who could help this family out.

They could have easily said no and in so doing missed out on one of the most incredible, joyful opportunities of their lives.

I asked Ty if he and Allison had to spend some time thinking it over. "Not at all," he said. "We were both ecstatic from that moment on. We were thrilled at the thought of providing these kids with what they had never experienced before—a family."

Things accelerated quickly. They immediately put their house on the market. "Within two hours after putting our house on the market, our phone rang. An agent wanted to see it. Within thirty-six hours, our house had sold at the full asking price." By the time the baby was a month old, Ty and Allison were the parents of four beautiful children.

Ty and Allison were called out of the blue to care for three orphaned children and were prepared to do so. I have no idea how God may call you to care for the orphan. My hope is that your heart is prepared as you have thought through what his Word says. May your passion for the fatherless flow from your love for God so that you are prepared to do whatever it is that God calls you to do to care for the fatherless. The need is clearly overwhelming. My prayer is that you are able to take the principles in God's Word and apply them for his glory!

AFTERWORD

If you're feeling anything like I did after reading *Passion for the Fatherless,* you're inspired, challenged, encouraged, humbled, and convicted—like you just got a "four-wheel spiritual alignment."

So where do we go from here?

Orphan ministry is challenging and messy. Do it anyway. You will not get all the affirmation, approval, and support you might like. Do it anyway. You will be overwhelmed as you consider the 100+ million orphaned and vulnerable children. Do it anyway.

When I consider the enormity of the task to which God has called his church, I am motivated by the words of Bob Pierce, founder of World Vision: "Don't fail to do something just because you can't do everything." As you strive to implement the biblical principles from this book, go deep in your care, but not so wide that you are unable to maximize your effectiveness.

And whenever you ever get that feeling of "What can I really do to make a difference?" take encouragement from a statement by Doug Sauder in *One Factor,* inspired by a saying in Kenya: "If you think you are too small to make a difference, you've never spent the night with a mosquito."

Here's a small glimpse into a few orphan ministry "ONE" factors I've seen:

- ONE pastor studied what the Bible has to say about the fatherless.
  Result: 30 children have been adopted or placed in foster homes, 28 people attended a mission trip to a Guatemalan orphanage, 7 adoption Bible studies were conducted, and a thriving ministry began at their church.
- ONE grandparent donated $10,000 to start an adoption fund.
  Result: 17 children have been adopted to date and the initial funds were used so wisely they have helped mobilize over $115,000 in adoption funding.

- ONE foster family in a church in Illinois adopted a malnourished and neglected baby named Bob.
  Result: Bob now runs a successful business and is giving his time, skills, and energy to help orphans know Jesus Christ as an orphan advocate.
- ONE couple in Irving, Texas, committed to starting an orphan ministry in their local church with limited resources.
  Result: thousands of adoptive families helped and adoption ministries begun at other local churches because of countless volunteer hours.
- ONE eight-year-old girl moved by hungry orphans in Zambia started putting up posters and raising money through small jobs.
  Result: 35 kids in her school were motivated to do the same, so 210 kids are now fed two meals each day, make joyful noises on a new playground, and have been introduced to Jesus Christ.

You can make a difference. We have an unprecedented breadth and depth of knowledge, endless supply of Christian resources, moving worship music . . . so much that we are privileged to digest (input), but comparatively so little by way of results and Kingdom fruit (output). Let's not just put this book on the shelf with good feelings and intentions. God invites us through James 1:22 to do the same: *"be doers of the Word, not hearers only."* Let's *do* this!

ANDY LEHMAN
Vice-President, Lifesong for Orphans

APPENDIX

---

1. Adapted from Lifesong for Orphan's application packet.

"OPEN HEARTS, OPEN HOMES"
ADOPTION APPLICATION

Husband's full name _____ DOB _____

Wife's full name _____ DOB _____

Street address _____

City _____

Home phone _____ Cell/work phone _____

E-mail address _____

Date of marriage _____

Husband's employer _____ Length of Employment _____

Wife's employer _____ Length of Employment _____

---

1. Prior divorce for husband   Y/N   If yes, date _____

2. Prior divorce for wife   Y/N   If yes, date _____

3. Names and ages of biological children in family _____

_____

_____

4. Have you adopted previously?   Y/N   If yes, list names/ages _____

_____

_____

5. Are you adopting domestically or internationally   D/I

6. If int'l, what country? _____   Have you completed your dossier   Y/N

7. Name of adoption agency _____

8. Do you have specific child identified
   already for this adoption   Y/N

If yes, full name _____   Age _____   Sex _____

9. Do you plan on adopting an
   older/special needs child?   Y/N

10. Member of (your church name)   Y/N   _____

PERSONAL STATEMENT OF FAITH

1. Who is God?

2. Who is Jesus Christ?

3. Who is the Holy Spirit?

4. How do you use God's Word (the Bible) in your life?

5. Describe your daily walk with God.

6. Describe your marital relationship.

7. Describe your church involvement.

8. What is eternal salvation? How does one receive eternal life?

9. Share your adoption testimony and describe how God has led you to adopt. (Please use a separate sheet of paper)

PARENTING PHILOSOPHY

Attach an additional sheet of paper if necessary to completely answer any questions.

What is your philosophy regarding the spiritual training of your children?

What is your philosophy regarding the education of your children?

Someday, your child will have questions about his/her life and existence. What will you teach your children about each of the following topics:

CREATION:

FALL:

REDEMPTION:

How would you describe your "parenting style"?

What types of discipleship training have you received to help you with your parenting? How do you plan to continue to improve your parenting skills?

What is your understanding of a covenant and your obligation to fulfill your part of a covenant that you make?

Describe your commitment to train your child to know and serve the Lord.

ADOPTION COSTS

Type of Expense	Amount	Due M/D/Y	Type of Expense	Amount	Due M/D/Y
Agency Fees	_____	_____	Overseas Fees	_____	_____
Child's Medical Exam	_____	_____	Translation Fees	_____	_____
Foreign Program Fee	_____	_____	Travel 1st Trip	_____	_____
Home Study	_____	_____	Travel 2nd Trip	_____	_____
In-Country Fees	_____	_____	Visas	_____	_____
INS Fees	_____	_____	Other	_____	_____
Orphanage Fees	_____	_____	Other	_____	_____
Notarization/ Authentication	_____	_____	TOTAL COST:	_____	_____

Please indicate how you intend to finance your adoption costs:

Personal Funds (savings, etc.) $ _____

Employer Benefit (if applicable) $ _____

Other Grants/Loans Applied For (list)

_____ $ _____

_____ $ _____

_____ $ _____

Other source of funds (please specify) $ _____

Total Estimated RESOURCES $ _____

Total Estimated Adoption COST $ _____

DEFICIT (Total Resources *minus* Total Cost) $ _____

Specify any special financial considerations or circumstances
we should be aware of:

NET WORTH

ASSETS

Cash

    On hand $ _____

    Checking $ _____

    Savings $ _____

Investments $ _____

Life Insurance (Cash Surrender Value, not death benefit) $ _____

Retirement Accounts $ _____

Personal Property

    Auto $ _____

    Auto $ _____

    Household $ _____

Real Estate

    Home $ _____

Other Assets $ _____

Total Assets $ _____

LIABILITIES

Current Bills $ _____

Credit Cards $ _____

Auto Loans $ _____

Home Mortgage $ _____

Other Liabilities $ _____

                            _____

Total Liabilities $ _____

Net Worth (Assets *minus* Liabilities) $ _____

CASH FLOW

	Monthly	Annual
Gross Income	$ _____	$ _____
Giving	$ _____	$ _____
Tax	$ _____	$ _____
Debt Repayment	$ _____	$ _____
(not including home mortgage)		
Net Spendable Income	$ _____	$ _____

(Total Gross Income *minus* Giving *minus* Taxes *minus* Debt)

Living Expenses

	Monthly	Annual
Housing		
Mortgage/Rent	$ _____	$ _____
Property Taxes	$ _____	$ _____
Insurance	$ _____	$ _____
Utilities	$ _____	$ _____
Other	$ _____	$ _____
Total Housing	$ _____	$ _____
Food	$ _____	$ _____
Clothing	$ _____	$ _____
Transportation	_____	_____
Car Payment	$ _____	$ _____
Insurance	$ _____	$ _____
Gas/Maintenance	$ _____	$ _____
Other	$ _____	$ _____
Total Transportation	$ _____	$ _____
Entertainment/Recreation	$ _____	$ _____
Medical Expenses	$ _____	$ _____
Insurance	$ _____	$ _____
Gifts	$ _____	$ _____
Miscellaneous	$ _____	$ _____
Total Living Expenses	$ _____	$ _____
Cash Flow	$ _____	$ _____

(Net Spendable Income *minus* Total Living Expenses)

CONSENT FORM

1. Purpose

The undersigned agrees that this application is being made for the purpose of obtaining assistance with adoption. The undersigned further acknowledges that the willingness to accept an application is not any type of acknowledgment or representation on behalf of Bethany Community Church that assistance will be granted or given.

2. Authorization and Release

The undersigned hereby authorizes any officer, employee, agent, representative, or staff member of Bethany Community Church and Lifesong to obtain financial and personal information from any institution or individual. The undersigned further consents to the release of any information to any authorized Bethany Community Church or Lifesong employee or agent from any individual or financial institution. The undersigned further authorizes any pastor, elder, minister, or counselor to release to Bethany Community Church or its representatives personal information and opinions regarding the applicant's lifestyle, language, habits, truthfulness, parental fitness, and general moral and biblical character. Please supply contact information below:

Adoption
Agency: _____

Case Worker: _____

Phone: _____

Additionally, please provide 2 character references, with one being a Bethany Community pastor or elder and the other being a Bethany Community church member (not related to you):

Name: _____   Phone: _____

Address: _____

Name: _____   Phone: _____

Address: _____

3. Limit of Liability

The undersigned acknowledges that Bethany Community Church has made no representation or warranty that financial aid or assistance will be furnished to the undersigned; and further acknowledges that Bethany Community Church shall have the sole discretion to accept or deny this application with or without cause. The undersigned further releases and holds Bethany Community Church harmless from any liability of any type or nature as a result of allowing the undersigned to submit this application.

4. Permission

The undersigned gives Bethany Community Church permission to use their story and/or photographs on Bethany Community Church's Web site and/or printed material (e.g., church bulletin, adoption ministry scrapbook, newsletter, etc.) for adoption ministry promotional purposes. (Your answer does not have an effect on financial assistance).

Yes_____ No_____

5. Support Raising Agreement

The undersigned parties acknowledge they are freely agreeing to the following terms and conditions as a requirement to participate in the adoption grant process for Bethany Community Church:

1. We will formulate a mailing list of supporters and mail a support letter to each one. The applicant pays the postage. Bethany Community Church will supply a Support Raising Kit which includes: (1) instructions for the process, (2) sample support letters, and (3) Bethany Community Church's letter of support on church letterhead stating the church's commitment to come alongside of an adopting couple.

2. We understand and accept that all funds and/or donations received by Bethany Community Church are under the ultimate control of Bethany Community Church. Bethany Community Church will make all final decisions regarding distributing and/or grants and loans of any funds.

3. We understand, accept, and agree to use any and all funds received by Bethany Community Church exclusively for legitimate adoption expenses, including but not limited to agency fees, legal fees, etc. We agree to provide verification of adoption related expenses to Bethany Community Church upon request.

4. We understand after our adoption support raising process, Bethany Community Church will make a determination how much of raised funds will be given as an interest-free loan, grant, or a combination of both.

5. We understand any funds raised (including the grant amount, if applicable) beyond our stated deficit will be used to further the ministry at Bethany Community Church and assist other families with the cost of adoption.

6. We understand we may not donate money to Bethany Community Church toward our own adoption expenses and receive a tax deduction.

7. We understand that if we decide not to adopt or our adoption is disrupted for any reason we will contact Bethany Community Church immediately. Any funds raised will be used to further the ministry of Bethany Community Church and assist other families with the cost of adoption. Donations cannot be returned to donors.

8. We agree to submit proper documentation as requested by Bethany Community Church for payment and/or reimbursements of any kind.

6. Attachments

1. *Picture* If you have a picture of the child you desire to adopt that you are willing to share with us, please include the photo along with this application.

2. *Copy of Home Study* Please include a copy of your home study with this application or when completed.

7. Signatures

We are providing this information to Bethany Community Church for their internal and confidential use. All information contained in this application is accurate to the best of our knowledge.

Adoptive Father: _____ Date: _____

Adoptive
Mother: _____ Date: _____

September 3, 2007

Dear Family and Friends of Daniel and Whitney Bennett,

Bethany Community Church is actively obeying the call of God in Scripture to care for the fatherless and the orphan. To facilitate this, Bethany has formed an adoption ministry, "Open Hearts, Open Homes," to assist families who are pursuing adoption or foster parenting in response to God's call to care for these children. Since Bethany's adoptive outreach is only just beginning, we are partnering with Lifesong for Orphans (www.lifesongfororphans. org), a non-profit Christian ministry dedicated to obeying God's call to "visit the fatherless ... in their affliction" (James 1:27).

The number of children worldwide without families to love and care for them is almost incomprehensible; experts estimate there are more than 60 million orphans around the world, children who need the love and compassion of parents and a family to transform their life.

God tells us in his Word that he hears the cry of the orphaned and abandoned children (Ps. 10:17–18), and he has made a way for them to be cared for through adoption. As believers, he has adopted us into his family through Jesus Christ and did not leave us as spiritual orphans!

We believe adoption at its core is evangelism, and a vital part of the Great Commission is bringing the mission field home. God desires orphans from all nations to be adopted into Christ-honoring families so they may ultimately be adopted into his eternal family through Jesus Christ. God calls all of us to care for orphans but he has not called all of us to adopt. Some are called to pray, some to give financially, some to visit orphanages on mission trips, and some to adopt.

The Bennetts have sensed God's call to adopt ... and have joyfully stepped out in faith and obedience to adopt a child from Guatemala. As you may already know, international adoption can cost $25,000 or more, and that prevents many godly families from adopting. Bethany and Life International believe God has raised up the Bennett family "for such a time as this," and we have committed to helping them in a variety of ways, including financially.

One of the ways Bethany is helping the Bennetts and others financially is by setting up a fund to which family and friends can contribute. If you would like to partner with Bethany to help the Bennetts raise the funds necessary to complete the adoption of this little child, please follow the instructions on the accompanying letter. All donations are tax deductible. *100% of all funds raised will go directly to cover adoption costs of families at Bethany Community; nothing will be taken out for Bethany Community Church's administrative costs.*

Will you invest financially in the life of this child? It will be an investment with an eternal return.

God bless you for laying up your treasures in heaven.

Sincerely,
Chuck Boysen
Open Hearts, Open Homes
Bethany Community Church Adoption Ministry

Dear Friends and Family,

In the spring of 2005, in my role as family pastor at Bethany Baptist Church, I began noticing that God was using foster parents in our church to reach children with the gospel in an amazing way. As I was struck by the effectiveness of a ministry that brought children into Christian homes, I tried to think of ways that our church could start a ministry that would encourage families to become foster parents. While I was thinking this through, Andy Lehman with Lifesong for Orphans contacted our church to see if he could meet with us to discuss his ministry. In June 2005, we met and Andy shared his vision for partnering with Bethany to begin an adoption ministry.

Originally, God called Whitney and me to help other families in the process of adoption and foster parenting by coming alongside of them. "Open Hearts, Open Homes," Bethany's adoption and foster ministry, began in the spring of 2006. As I presented the ministry to others in our church, I was surprised at how the Lord had already been working in the hearts of his people to do his work. We held several well-attended informational meetings and started a Bible study with nine couples. The study lasted ten weeks and by its conclusion five of the couples were in the process of adopting.

As Whitney and I went through the Bible study, several things happened. First, we became more aware of the need for Christians to step forward and care for these little ones. Second, we began to see the fulfillment of the vision to have people from Bethany bringing young ones from all over the country and the world into their homes to hear the good news of Jesus Christ. Finally, God showed us how we might be able to adopt ourselves.

All this to say: *We're expecting ... to adopt!* Recently, as "Open Hearts, Open Homes," began planning a mission trip to an orphanage in Guatemala, Whitney and I saw God calling us to adopt a child through this orphanage. We are excited about this ministry and cannot wait to see what God is going to do in our lives, the lives of people in our church, the lives of our current children, and especially in the life of our future little one.

Originally, the exciting part of "Open Hearts, Open Homes" was that it allowed us to come alongside others who were in the process of adopting and be a part of bringing a little one into a Christian home. If this sounds exciting to you as well, prayerfully consider how God might have you involved in this ministry. We are estimating that the adoption costs will be between $25,000 and $30,000. Perhaps he would have you pray for us, or financially support us, or even work in your church to meet the needs of little ones.

By his Grace,
Daniel, Whitney, Hannah, Austin, and Noah Bennett

P.S. For updates on our adoption process, you can visit our blog at:
http://danielbennett.blogspot.com.

WORKS CITED

Alcorn, Randy. *Money, Possessions, and Eternity.* Wheaton, IL: Tyndale, 2003.

Allen, Ronald B. "Psalm 87: A Song Rarely Sung." *Bibliotheca Sacra* 153 (April–June 1996): 131–40.

Austen, Jane. *Mansfield Park.* In *The Complete Novels.* New York: Penguin Books, 2006.

Bock, Darrell. *Luke,* Volume 1: 1:1–9:50. Baker Exegetical Commentary on the New Testament. Grand Rapids: Baker Books, 1994.

Brooks, Arthur. *Who Really Cares: The Surprising Truth about Compassionate Conservatism.* New York: Basic Books, 2006.

Calvin, John. *Institutes of the Christian Religion.* Grand Rapids: Eerdmans, 1989.

Christianbook.com. "Interview with Brian McLaren." http://www.christianbook.com/Christian/Books/cms_content/658134109?page=178 0620&event=1010SBF|1780620 (accessed February 25, 2010).

Corbett, Steve and Brian Fikkert. *When Helping Hurts: How to Alleviate Poverty Without Hurting the Poor and Yourself.* Chicago: Moody Publishers, 2009.

DeYoung, Kevin. *Just Do Something: A Liberating Approach to Finding God's Will.* Chicago: Moody Press, 2009.

Gardner, Michelle. *After the Dream Comes True.* Enumclaw, WA: Pleasant Word Publishing, 2004.

Green, Joel. *The Gospel of Luke.* Grand Rapids: Eerdmans, 1997.

Grudem, Wayne. *Systematic Theology.* Grand Rapids: Zondervan, 1994.

Hipps, Shane. *Flickering Pixels: How Technology Shapes Your Faith.* Grand Rapids: Zondervan, 2009).

Hoehner, Harold W. *Ephesians: An Exegetical Commentary.* Grand Rapids: Baker, 2002.

Huffman, Douglas S., ed. *How Then Should We Choose: Three Views on God's Will and Decision Making.* Grand Rapids: Kregel, 2009.

Keller, Timothy J. *Ministries of Mercy.* Phillipsburg, NJ: P & R Publishing, 1997.

MacDonald, James. *Way of Wisdom: Finding Direction in God's Will*. Grand Rapids: Walk in the Word, 2007.

Metzger, Will. *Tell the Truth*. Downer's Grove, IL: InterVarsity Press, 2002.

Miller, Lisa. "An Evangelical Identity Crisis." *Newsweek*, November 13, 2006. http://www.newsweek.com/id/44547/page/1 (accessed February 25, 2010).

Moore, Russell D. *Adopted for Life: The Priority of Adoption for Christian Families & Churches*. Wheaton, IL: Crossway, 2009.

Murphy, Caryle "Evangelical Author Puts Progressive Spin on Traditional Faith." *The Washington Post*, September 10, 2006. http://www.washingtonpost.com/wp-dyn/content/article/2006/09/09/AR2006090901155.html (accessed February 25, 2010).

Murray, Ian H. *Evangelicalism Divided*. Carlisle, PA: Banner of Truth, 2000.

Packer, J. I. *Knowing God*. Wheaton, IL: InterVarsity Press, 1993.

Parish, Peggy. *Amelia Bedelia*. New York, NY: HarperCollins, 1963.

Paulson, Michael. "Rob Bell on Faith, Suffering, and Christians." *Boston Globe*, September 26, 2009. http://www.boston.com/news/local/articles_of_faith/2009/09/rob_bell.html (accessed October 6, 2009).

Piper, John. *Let the Nations Be Glad*. Grand Rapids: Baker Academic, 2003.

————— and Wayne Grudem. "What Does the Bible Say About Leadership in the Church?" Council for Biblical Manhood and Womanhood. https://www.cbmw.org/FAQs/Questions-and-Answers/What-does-the-Bible-say-about-leadership-in-the-church (accessed March 14, 2010).

Strauch, Alexander. *Biblical Eldership: An Urgent Call to Restore Biblical Church Leadership*. Littleton, CO: Lewis & Roth.

Ten Boom, Corrie. *Tramp for the Lord*. Fort Washington, PA: Christian Literature Crusade; Old Tappan, NJ: 1974.

UNICEF. "Child Protection," http://www.unicef.org/media/media_45451.html (accessed July 11, 2009).

—————. "Child Survival and Development." http://www.unicef.org/media/media_45485.html (accessed July 11, 2009).

—————. "HIV and AIDS." http://www.unicef.org/media/media_45486.html (accessed July 11, 2009).

—————. "Orphans." http://www.unicef.org/media/media_45290.html (accessed July 12, 2009).

—————. "Water, Sanitation, and Hygiene." http://www.unicef.org/media/media_4581.html (accessed July 11, 2009).

Waltke, Bruce. *Finding the Will of God*. Grand Rapids: Eerdmans, 1995.

Ware, Bruce. *Father, Son, and Holy Spirit: Relationships, Roles and Relevance*. Wheaton, IL: Crossway, 2005.

Wells, David. *The Courage to Be Protestant*. Grand Rapids: Eerdmans, 2008.

————. *No Place for Truth, or, Whatever Happened to Evangelical Theology.* Grand Rapids: Eerdmans, 1993.

Whitney, Donald S. *Ten Questions to Diagnose Your Spiritual Health.* Colorado Springs: NavPress, 2001.

Wiesel, Elie. *Night.* New York: Hill and Wang, 2006.

Williams, David. "Is Your Desk Making You Sick?" CNN.com, November 13, 2006. http://www.cnn.com/2004/HEALTH/12/13/cold.flu.desk /index.html (accessed November 9, 2009).

SCRIPTURE INDEX

SUBJECT INDEX